The British Constitution: A Very Short Introduction

VERY SHORT INTRODUCTIONS are for anyone wanting a stimulating and accessible way in to a new subject. They are written by experts, and have been published in more than 25 languages worldwide.

The series began in 1995, and now represents a wide variety of topics in history, philosophy, religion, science, and the humanities. The VSI Library now contains more than 300 volumes—a Very Short Introduction to everything from ancient Egypt and Indian philosophy to conceptual art and cosmology—and will continue to grow in a variety of disciplines.

Very Short Introductions available now:

ADVERTISING Winston Fletcher
AFRICAN HISTORY
   John Parker and Richard Rathbone
AGNOSTICISM Robin Le Poidevin
AMERICAN HISTORY Paul S. Boyer
AMERICAN IMMIGRATION
   David A. Gerber
AMERICAN POLITICAL PARTIES
   AND ELECTIONS L. Sandy Maisel
THE AMERICAN PRESIDENCY
   Charles O. Jones
ANAESTHESIA Aidan O'Donnell
ANARCHISM Colin Ward
ANCIENT EGYPT Ian Shaw
ANCIENT GREECE Paul Cartledge
ANCIENT PHILOSOPHY Julia Annas
ANCIENT WARFARE
   Harry Sidebottom
ANGELS David Albert Jones
ANGLICANISM Mark Chapman
THE ANGLO-SAXON AGE John Blair
THE ANIMAL KINGDOM
   Peter Holland
ANIMAL RIGHTS David DeGrazia
THE ANTARCTIC Klaus Dodds
ANTISEMITISM Steven Beller
ANXIETY
   Daniel Freeman and Jason Freeman
THE APOCRYPHAL GOSPELS
   Paul Foster
ARCHAEOLOGY Paul Bahn
ARCHITECTURE Andrew Ballantyne
ARISTOCRACY William Doyle
ARISTOTLE Jonathan Barnes

ART HISTORY Dana Arnold
ART THEORY Cynthia Freeland
ATHEISM Julian Baggini
AUGUSTINE Henry Chadwick
AUSTRALIA Kenneth Morgan
AUTISM Uta Frith
THE AVANT-GARDE David Cottington
THE AZTECS David Carrasco
BARTHES Jonathan Culler
BEAUTY Roger Scruton
BESTSELLERS John Sutherland
THE BIBLE John Riches
BIBLICAL ARCHAEOLOGY
   Eric H. Cline
BIOGRAPHY Hermione Lee
THE BLUES Elijah Wald
THE BOOK OF MORMON
   Terryl Givens
BORDERS
   Alexander C. Diener and Joshua Hagen
THE BRAIN Michael O'Shea
THE BRITISH CONSTITUTION
   Martin Loughlin
BRITISH POLITICS Anthony Wright
BUDDHA Michael Carrithers
BUDDHISM Damien Keown
BUDDHIST ETHICS Damien Keown
CANCER Nicholas James
CAPITALISM James Fulcher
CATHOLICISM Gerald O'Collins
THE CELL
   Terence Allen and Graham Cowling
THE CELTS Barry Cunliffe
CHAOS Leonard Smith

Available soon:

For more information visit our website

www.oup.com/vsi

Martin Loughlin

THE BRITISH CONSTITUTION

A Very Short Introduction

OXFORD
UNIVERSITY PRESS

OXFORD
UNIVERSITY PRESS

Great Clarendon Street, Oxford, OX2 6DP,
United Kingdom

Oxford University Press is a department of the University of Oxford.
It furthers the University's objective of excellence in research, scholarship,
and education by publishing worldwide. Oxford is a registered trade mark of
Oxford University Press in the UK and in certain other countries

British Library Cataloguing in Publication Data

Data available

ISBN 978-0-19-969769-4

Printed in Great Britain by
Ashford Colour Press Ltd, Gosport, Hampshire

Contents

Contents

Acknowledgements

For some years there has been the absence of an introduction to the British constitution that explains how it has evolved, how it all seemed to make sense, and how during the modern era it has veered from being a major source of pride to an arrangement that provokes dissatisfaction. The chance of filling that gap myself arose after I took on the role of Head of Department: since the job leaves little time for original research and scholarship, here at least was an excuse for abandoning the conventional scaffolding of academic writing and 'shooting from the hip'. Inevitably, it did not turn out to be as straightforward as I had anticipated. In helping me to keep on track, I owe a particular debt to my co-teachers in LSE's public law course: Conor Gearty, Jo Murkens, Thomas Poole, and Grégoire Webber all read and commented on the draft and they have done their best to save me from some of my more egregious errors and distortions. I have also benefited from feedback from OUP's two readers. Finally, for once again showing me how to express my at times complicated views on this subject in a more direct and simple style, I am pleased to record my thanks to Chris Foley.

List of illustrations

Introduction

Once extolled as a standing wonder, the British constitution today can evoke bewilderment and sometimes even derision. Many now find the idea of a constitution that has grown organically in response to economic, political, and social changes rather puzzling. A century ago, Sidney Low claimed that although 'we live under a system of tacit understandings...the understandings themselves are not always understood'. Today the problem is not confined to grasping the meaning of these tacit understandings of the constitution: the question is whether they can be said still to exist.

The British clearly have a system of government, a set of rules regulating the exercise of political power. But the idea of a 'constitution' connotes something more. It implies that institutions of government are infused with values and with modes of conduct that fix the meaning of those rules and, in doing so, express a political way of being. Do such values and practices still exist in the British system and if so do they still command authority? It is in this deeper sense that we ask whether a British constitution can still be said to exist.

There is every reason to answer that question affirmatively, not least because this book would otherwise rank as the shortest of all

Very Short Introductions. But the evidence of the last thirty or so years is not reassuring. Consider this snapshot of the period.

From the 1970s, we might pick Lord Hailsham's celebrated 1976 Dimbleby Lecture on *Elective Dictatorship*. Beginning with the paradox that government had never before possessed so much power and commanded so little respect, he noted that there was scarcely an institution of government nowadays that does not come in for serious criticism. For Hailsham, this was because these institutions were no longer performing their constitutional role of providing an implicit balancing mechanism: the monarchy had been reduced to an entirely ceremonial function, the House of Lords no longer acted as a restraining influence, and political conduct in general seemed to be dictated by party political interest rather than any sense of appropriate behaviour on the part of officeholders. Customary constitutional restraints were no longer working, leading to a loss of trust. More broadly, the traditions of civility from which these constitutional values grew were losing authority. The only solution, Hailsham concluded, was to devise an entirely new constitution. Like all new constitutions, this would be written down and be defined by law.

Hailsham was as far removed from being a radical as one might find: son of a viscount, educated at Eton and Oxford, after practising at the bar he had a successful career as a Conservative MP and Minister. His analysis of the failures of the traditional constitution might have had something to do with the widespread conviction of the time that the Labour party was 'the natural party of government'. When the Conservatives were returned to office in 1979, Hailsham, now Lord Chancellor, quietly shelved his radical proposal. Anyway, the Conservatives had other fish to fry—reducing the powers of government seemed more important than reforming the constitution. But Hailsham's theme was immediately taken up by a breakaway Labour group who in 1981 founded a new party, the Social Democratic Party. At the heart of the SDP's programme was a proposal for fundamental constitutional reform.

The case was elaborated by their constitutional guru, David Marquand. In *The Unprincipled Society* (1988), Marquand argued that Britain's problems—economic as well as political—stemmed from the failure of its political class to shed a Victorian constitutional mentality. His thesis was more radical than Hailsham's: whereas Hailsham proposed a modern constitution in order to protect the Victorian values that Conservatives hold dear, Marquand was criticizing their pervasive influence. The problem was that we were living in a society in which property rights were antecedent to society, liberty was realized only when we were left alone, and government was best left in the hands of an experienced political elite conscious of its obligations to society. Far from being a symbol of British genius, the traditional constitution was the source of our present weaknesses. For Marquand, the British problem was one of maladaptation and, in order to promote modern ideas of democracy and citizenship rights, the first step must be fundamental constitutional reform.

This message was soon picked up by Labour. During the 1990s, the Labour party reformed itself and, rebranded as 'new Labour', won the 1997 election on a platform of constitutional modernization. It immediately introduced new measures of constitutional significance: governmental power was devolved to Scotland, Wales, and Northern Ireland, the House of Lords was reformed, and reforming measures such as the Human Rights Act and the Freedom of Information Act were enacted. New Labour promoted a more radical set of constitutional reforms than any government since the First World War.

But the delivery of these reforms provoked unsettling questions. Wasn't this package rather makeshift? Was the vision of a new constitutional settlement coherent? Didn't these reforms leave untouched the exercise of power at the centre? Did they not in fact demonstrate the impossibility of governments themselves reordering constitutional fundamentals? Will Hutton had already indicated the difficulties. In *The State We're In* (1995), he explained how economic and political changes since the 1970s had eroded the public service ethos that had bolstered traditional arrangements. But he also recognized that the sort of fundamental constitutional reform now required had never before been achieved by any nation without the utter collapse of its system of government. Trust in governing institutions had been progressively weakened without any signs of the public realm being restored.

We seem now to have reached an impasse. Continuing economic and political development—of which globalization and European integration are particularly important manifestations—has required the overthrow of many traditional practices, and successive governments, Conservative as well as Labour, have sought to modernize governing arrangements and codify its rules. But all this has been taking place without addressing the first principles of fundamental reform. We are all modernizers now. Even the Conservative-dominated Coalition Government formed in 2010 has furthered the cause with provisions such as the Parliamentary Voting System and Constituencies Act 2011, authorizing a referendum on a more proportionate voting system and promoting the equalization in size (and reduction in number) of parliamentary constituencies. The fact that this voting reform was rejected by the electorate is of secondary importance. The critical point is that the entire political class seems to have lost faith in customary ways of governing. By tinkering with the rules they present themselves as 'modern'. Yet incremental modernization has merely blurred the issue. We have in some haphazard way codified many of the rules and in that sense are closer than ever to having a 'written constitution', but at the same time we no longer have a clear sense of the values of the public realm that this rule-system is supposed to protect and promote.

So what can a short introduction to the British constitution hope to deliver? In the light of contemporary uncertainties, the only sound approach is to offer an explanation of how we have arrived at our present state. Without understanding that history we have no hope of grasping our present constitutional predicament. The aim is not to study the past for its own sake: it is to sketch one strand of what in 2010 the Secretary of State for Education called 'our island story'. We should, however, be clear that even this strand of 'our island story' cannot be presented as a linear and coherent narrative and, since it does not run a straight course, the reader should assume that any apparent repetition is deliberate! Most importantly, the story cannot be told in terms that celebrate the genius that made 'the matchless constitution'. If we are to acquire an understanding of the terms of the governing relationship—and the ways that relationship is bound up in the nation's collective identity—then that historical experience has to be presented in a dispassionate manner.

The book begins, then, by outlining the character of the traditional constitution with a view to explaining how it survived into the modern world. Why, when all other nations were adopting formal documentary statements of their constitutional arrangements, did the British maintain these traditional arrangements? In later chapters, in which current practices are outlined, I try to situate them within a tradition of conduct and with an eye on the critical questions. What particular strains are experienced when operating in the modern world of government with a heritage of traditional constitutional forms? How well have these British arrangements been able to adapt? What forces are shaping present and future governmental developments? Only when we have addressed these questions can we ask the basic question: does Britain today possess a constitution?

Chapter 1
What constitution?

The full, the perfect plan
Of Britain's matchless constitution, mixt
Of mutual checking and supporting powers,
Kings, Lords, and Commons

James Thomson, *Liberty*, 1736.

In England the constitution may change continually, or
rather it does not in reality exist.

Alexis de Tocqueville, *Democracy in America*, 1835.

The matchless constitution?

During the 18th century the British constitution was extolled as
the 'matchless constitution', combining the virtues of monarchy,
aristocracy, and democracy while avoiding their characteristic
vices. But the British seem to have lost faith in this historic
constitution. Once admired for its ability to effect the transition to
modern parliamentary democracy by incremental adjustment
without the need for violent revolution, the British constitution is
today seen in many quarters to be reaching its terminus. The need
for 'constitutional modernization' or 'constitutional renewal' has
become a regular refrain among today's political class. But the
urge for renewal is invariably tinged with pathos, a melancholy,
long, withdrawing roar—a loss of faith, even of meaning.

Constitutionally speaking, we are living through a period of considerable uncertainty.

This book focuses on the historical tropes through which the British have sought to explain and justify their governing arrangements and through which they have created a distinctive political identity. We begin with some preliminary reflections on the character of the British constitution. The British are regarded throughout the world as almost unique in not having a 'written' constitution. What does this mean? It cannot mean that governing arrangements are not laid down in writing. If by constitution we mean the rules that establish and regulate the institutions of government, then the British possess a set of such rules. In this sense, the only unusual feature of the British constitution is that these rules have not been gathered together in a document called 'the Constitution'. Is this the deficiency contemporary reformers seek to remedy? Is constitutional modernization driven only by the desire to systematize these rules and present them in a single document?

That would be an over-simplification. The difficulties touch on more fundamental questions that concern not just the effectiveness but the legitimacy of Britain's governing arrangements. The term 'constitution' itself is ambiguous, so is it possible that the current dissatisfaction stems from uncertainty over its meaning?

In the history of political constitutions some discrepancy has arisen between what have been called traditional and modern understandings. Since the British have a historic, customary, evolutionary—i.e. traditional—constitution, we begin by considering this distinction.

The traditional idea of the constitution

Writing in 1830, the great German philosopher G. W. F. Hegel claimed that 'what is called "making" a "constitution" is a thing that has never happened in history'. The constitution of a state, he was arguing, is not merely a set of institutional arrangements; it is a cultural artefact and it 'develops from the national spirit'. In this traditional understanding of the term, the constitution expresses a nation's culture, customs, and values just as much as its system of government. The constitution is certainly not some dish that can be made from a recipe. It can no more be made than language is made; like language, the constitution evolves through usage. It expresses the ways in which we conceive ourselves as a 'people' or a 'nation' or, when focusing on our governing arrangements, as a 'state'.

One of the greatest exponents of this traditional sense of the constitution was Edmund Burke. Burke's views are most famously expressed in *Reflections on the Revolution in France* (1790), the purpose of which was to warn the French of the dangers of engaging in radical constitutional reconstruction in the wake of the 1789 Revolution. A political constitution, Burke argues, is 'an entailed inheritance' derived from 'our forefathers' and transmitted to posterity. It is 'a liberal descent': we respect institutions established over time and seek to improve them incrementally, but if they are not entirely obsolete we also seek to retain them. Only through such prudent and incremental reform can we 'bind up the constitution of our country with our dearest domestic ties, and adopt our fundamental laws into the bosom of our family affections'. Only by working within the grain of social and political development can the constitution become a living reality.

Burke's most basic point is that when constitution-making is reduced to a rationalist exercise in construction, all the 'pleasing illusions which made power gentle and obedience liberal' are dissolved. If 'ancient opinions and rules of life are taken away', the loss is inestimable. We no longer have a compass to govern us, we cannot know in which direction to steer, and we fall into a condition of ceaseless change. His claim is that constitutional government works not because of the symmetry of some formal rule-based design but through the gradual emergence of customary ways of conduct that channel the exercise of power through certain ceremonies and forms. Strip away the mystique and you remove the behavioural constraints that make the exercise of governing power benign. Remove the sacred from the constitutional and 'the whole chain and continuity of the commonwealth' is broken. Treat the state as a mechanism that can be made and re-made in accordance with the 'floating fancies or fashions' and we lose the very basis of political authority.

For Burke, the task of maintaining the constitution of a state requires a most delicate skill. It requires a grasp of human nature and human necessities, together with knowledge of what facilitates or obstructs the various ends pursued by governing institutions. It is a practical art that draws on the experience of a governing elite and is acquired through traditions handed down over many generations. This is not a task to be devised from some philosophical template. The constitution is 'a partnership not only between those who are living, but between those who are living, those who are dead, and those who are to be born'. Indeed, in this traditional understanding, the better the constitution the fewer the written constitutional laws, since laws only reinforce a mode of conduct that has not been fully absorbed in the manners, traditions, and practices of a people.

The modern idea of the constitution

With the benefit of hindsight, it might be said that Hegel was wrong on the subject of 'making' constitutions. During the summer of 1787 delegates from the thirteen American states met in Philadelphia to discuss and draft a new Federal Constitution for the United States of America. 'After the lapse of 6,000 years since the creation of the world', wrote James Wilson, 'America now presents the first instance of a people assembled to weigh deliberately and calmly, to decide leisurely and peaceably, upon the form of government by which they will bind themselves and their posterity.' The US Constitution of 1787 became the world's first modern written constitution. Its adoption opened a new era in constitutional development. Thereafter, at certain critical points in their history, nations began to adopt constitutions in the form of specific texts that laid down the framework of their governing institutions.

The founders of the modern American republic were conscious of the fact that they were making a new type of constitution. In the first of *The Federalist Papers*, the journalistic effort by leading framers to persuade the voters of New York to ratify the new Constitution, Alexander Hamilton observed that it was 'reserved to the people of this country' to decide whether societies are 'capable or not of establishing good government from reflection and choice' or whether they were 'destined to depend for their political constitutions on accident and force'. In place of the idea that the constitution expressed a nation's traditions and ethical practices, Hamilton was arguing that the traditional idea rested on vagaries of 'accident and force', on power interests rather than cultural commitments. Contrary to Burke's assertion, Hamilton contended that the constitution was not simply an 'inheritance' or set of practices consecrated by custom and received by a people; it was an instrument by which 'the people', after rational debate, agree the terms on which they are governed.

Thomas Paine immediately recognized the revolutionary nature of the shift taking place. 'It is not sufficient that we adopt the word', he declaimed, 'we must fix also a standard specification to it.' In his *Rights of Man* of 1791, Paine provided the first clear statement of the modern idea of a constitution. A constitution, he argued, must possess four key features:

1. It must have a real rather than virtual existence; a constitution is a thing and, specifically, a *document*.

2. The constitution is a thing *antecedent to a government*. Since it establishes the government, it cannot be made by government, but only by 'the people'.

3. The constitution must fully specify the powers and duties of the government: it must be *comprehensive*.

4. The constitution has the status of *fundamental law*. Being the law of law-making, the constitution is a higher form of law: since this body of constitutional law is not made by the governing institutions but by the people to establish those institutions, governments and legislatures have no authority to alter constitutional law.

This modern concept of a constitution has since been adopted across the world. Nearly 200 nation-states, along with many sub-national units (provinces, states, etc.) in federal regimes, now have written constitutions of the modern type—documents that define and limit the powers of the institutions of government and which take effect as fundamental law.

Traditional v. modern

Modern constitutions possess varying degrees of authority. It would certainly be wrong to take the US Constitution as the epitome of the modern concept. Drafted in 1787, it has since 1791, when the first ten Amendments were attached as the Bill of Rights, been amended only seventeen times and is now regarded as set in stone. By contrast, the French have adopted at least twelve different constitutions since their Revolution of 1789 and have experienced dictatorship, monarchy, and five republics. The French experience is more typical. Only a handful of national constitutions pre-date the Second World War and the vast majority of current constitutions have been adopted, or fundamentally amended, in the last thirty years.

This variable experience should caution against any assumption that the modern concept of constitution as text has altogether replaced the traditional idea. Standards for governmental decision-making laid down in written constitutions express ideal aspirations but they often tell us little about the way power is being exercised in that regime. Indeed, the constitution may simply be a façade that masks stark realities. But even if the norms laid down in the text are fully complied with, it should be emphasized that they only regulate the office of government. Behind the shadow lies the substance: behind *government* lies the *state* itself—the way we conceive the political unity of a people.

The essential point is that the traditional and modern concepts have different objects: the modern constitution has as its object the office of government, while the traditional concept has that of the state. The modern concept distinguishes between government and society, whereas the traditional concept suggests that the manners, culture, and traditions of a people form the 'real' constitution of the state.

Experience indicates that the task of drafting a constitution of the modern type is not so difficult. Though they come in different styles, they tend to follow a common template. The US Constitution remains a model of concision: the first article establishes a national bicameral legislature (the Congress); the second, a national executive (the President); the third, a national judicature (the Supreme Court); the fourth, the relationship with the states; the fifth, the amending procedure; the sixth, the treatment of public debt; and the seventh (and last) the procedure for ratification. But drafting and adopting such a constitution does not make it a living reality. That task lies ahead.

The great challenge for states adopting a new constitutional settlement is to ensure that its principles and values are embraced by its people. The challenge is to foster a political culture that upholds the status of the constitution. The case of 20th-century Germany is particularly instructive. The social democratic Weimar Constitution of 1919 failed because, in the fraught circumstances of defeat in the First World War and the removal of the monarchy, many political parties refused to accept the authority of the new constitution. One of the great achievements of the German people in the post-Second World War period has been to live up to the values and procedures of the federal constitution that was effectively imposed on them by the Allies after the war.

Modern constitutions, it is evident, serve both instrumental and symbolic purposes. As instruments of government they guide and control the various procedures of public decision-making. As symbolic documents, they excite reverence and offer a symbol of unity and identity. In their instrumental role, they are geared to the future and the shaping of subsequent political action, but in their symbolic function they draw on the past and in particular their stock of heroic stories about the vicissitudes of a virtuous people. These 'mere scraps of paper' are transformed into authoritative—almost sacred—texts only if both aspects are aligned. This suggests that the constitution can fully realize its ambition only when it functions in harmony with the customs of the people. The constitution of the office of government (the modern idea) must be consonant with that of the constitution of the state (the traditional idea).

The traditional constitution may be less precise with respect to instrumental guidance; after all, it generally draws on custom and practice rather than formally promulgated rules. But these evolving practices reflect changes in the political culture of the nation, which can radically alter the character of formal constitutional settlements. In this sense, the 'real' constitution of the United States—the ways in which power is today legitimately exercised in practice—might be just as unwritten as that of the United Kingdom.

Why does Britain not possess a modern constitution?

The British are almost unique in retaining a constitution of the traditional type. But because the modern concept is now so prevalent, it is widely assumed that the British do not even possess a constitution. The fact that the British constitution cannot be found in a single document and that laws relating to the constitution of government can be repealed or amended by Act of Parliament in exactly the same way as ordinary laws does not meant that the constitution does not exist. This view was being openly expressed even in the early 19th century. 'In England the constitution may change continually', noted Tocqueville in 1835, and he went on to suggest that 'it does not in reality exist'. Why does Britain not possess a constitution of the modern type?

The modern concept of the constitution is the product of the Enlightenment, a movement that flourished throughout western Europe during the mid- to late 18th century. Sometimes called 'the Age of Reason', the Enlightenment was an expression of a secular, scientific, rationalist spirit that left its mark on the arts, the sciences, religion, and politics. Its imprint—especially in its aspiration of freedom from arbitrary power—can be seen on both the American and French revolutions.

Since the late 18th century, modern constitutions have been adopted by many nations at critical moments in their history, largely as a consequence of some major crisis that has shaken the foundations of governmental authority. Modern constitutions have therefore been most commonly drafted in the aftermath of defeat in war or on the success of a revolutionary movement in overthrowing the old order, or because of the formation of new states as a result of the break-up of old empires. They symbolize the opening of a new chapter in the nation's history or the birth of a new nation-state.

As it happens, since the 18th century the British have managed to make the transition to modernity without revolutionary insurrection. Indeed, some might say that this is precisely because of the flexibility of their traditional constitution. They have also been fortunate not to have suffered the ignominy of defeat in war.

Consequently, while British lawyers have acquired considerable experience in drafting constitutions for former colonies that have obtained independence since the Second World War, they have never had occasion to examine their own constitutional fundamentals and codify the British constitution in a single authoritative document.

An alternative way of looking at this history might be to note that the British—strictly, the English—had their political revolution too early. In English political history, the era of revolutionary upheaval was the 17th rather than the 18th century. During the 1640s civil war raged in England and after the defeat of the Royalist cause in 1649 the king—Charles I—was executed and a Commonwealth formed. During this latter period, a written constitution was actually drawn up. The Instrument of Government of 1653, which created new governing arrangements by placing legislative power in Parliament and executive power in a Lord Protector (Cromwell) and his Council, might be viewed as the first written constitution of a modern nation-state. But this constitution did not establish a comprehensive framework of government and for this reason it cannot be viewed as a constitution of the modern type. The governing arrangements that were instituted also suggested that the revolutionaries who were responsible for executing the king still believed in the office of the king. Attempts to persuade Cromwell to assume the crown were unsuccessful and arrangements quickly unravelled after his death in 1658. In 1660 the dominant faction restored the monarchy by inviting Charles II to take his father's throne.

A further upheaval occurred in 1688. In 1685, Charles II was succeeded by his younger brother, James. James II wanted to institute a programme of absolutist Catholic modernization modelled on the French regime of Louis XIV. Faced with this threat to the traditional constitution, the Whig aristocracy enlisted the help of William of Orange, who was married to James's Protestant daughter Mary. When William landed in

England at the head of a Dutch army, James fled the country. The ruling elite determined that James had forfeited the crown. They then held a convention Parliament without the king who should have summoned it and invited William and Mary to reign jointly.

Once again, the terms of this new constitutional settlement were drafted in a formal document. But the Bill of Rights of 1689 was merely the statement of a resolution of grievances that Parliament held against the actions of government. The events of 1688 actually mark the world's first modern revolution. Yet the Bill of Rights, while not amounting itself to a modern constitution, did pave the way for a modern constitutional arrangement based on what might be called a parliamentary state. The significance of 1688 is complicated by the fact that the language of the revolutionary settlement was thoroughly conservative: the settlement was presented as the restoration of the traditional constitution whose workings had been undermined by the actions of the Stuart kings. In reality, it amounted to an aristocratic coup d'état and it resulted in the balance of power shifting from crown to Parliament. In masking this fact, the language of the 1688 settlement set the tone of subsequent discourse: thereafter, modernizing changes were invariably dressed up in a rhetoric of constitutional conservation.

Since the 17th century, there has been no fundamental breakdown in governmental authority that would cause the English to reconstitute themselves politically. But this does not mean there have been no basic changes in the structure of the state. Since the 17th century, we have seen the transformation of England into the state of Great Britain in 1707, and then in 1800 the formation of the United Kingdom of Great Britain and Ireland, and after 1920 the United Kingdom of Great Britain and Northern Ireland.

The United Kingdom now forms a complex, pluri-national state. The English state was centralized as a result of the Norman

Conquest of 1066, and thereafter the key strategic objective of the Normans was to maintain the security of England's borders by subjugating the other nations of the British Isles. With respect to Wales, this process was complete by 1535 when Wales was absorbed into the English shire structure: the English state incorporated Wales, and the English common law was applied throughout England and Wales. The position with respect to Scotland and Ireland is less simple. Scotland was not conquered; instead, in 1707 England entered into the Treaty of Union with Scotland to form the state of Great Britain. Relations with Ireland are even more complicated, but all that need be said at the moment is that the Union with Ireland Act 1800 abolished the Irish Parliament and provided for Irish representation in the new Parliament of the United Kingdom of Great Britain and Ireland. On each occasion, these treaties formally established a new state. Why, then, did they not lead to a modern constitutional settlement?

Consider the Scottish case. The Treaty of Union provided for Scottish representation in the English Parliament and contained protections for aspects of Scots public identity, especially law, Church, and education. There has recently developed in Scotland a romantic view that this is in fact a constitutional treaty in the modern sense. But the evidence suggests that it was essentially an incorporating exercise: the effect of the Treaty was to incorporate Scotland into the governing framework of the English state. Those who suggest otherwise are making a historically anachronistic argument: to read the Treaty of 1707 through post-Enlightenment constitutional spectacles is both bad politics and bad law. In engineering this union, the English deliberately avoided—for reasons of state—opening up for consideration any fundamental constitutional questions.

The policy of the English governing class with respect to the Anglo-Scottish Union indicates one reason why governmental developments since the 17th century have never resulted in constitutional renewal: the English governing temperament has always militated against any serious enquiry into the first principles of constitutional practice. The vagaries of historical development provide one explanation of why a modern constitution has not been adopted, but it is less than comprehensive. We should also consider the temperament of the English.

The spirit of the British constitution

It is often said that the distinctive virtue of the English is their fixation on the practical, while their distinctive vice is an unwillingness to gauge their achievements in terms of principle. The English—and indeed British—maintain an empiricist and pragmatic disposition. Suspicion of abstract speculation threads its way through the traditions of British philosophy from Bacon, Hobbes, and Locke to Hume, Bentham, and Mill. It is rooted in uncompromising matter-of-factness, a tendency to weigh up knowledge against utility. This pragmatic and anti-Rationalist temperament has left its imprint on matters of politics, government, and constitution.

Burke is a great exemplar of this disposition. In his essay on the French Revolution, he contended that the British constitution, as with all true constitutions, had been sustained by a distrust of abstract principles. Political institutions, he argued, are too complex to be governed according to principles that take no account of time, place, or circumstance. Politics must be adapted 'not to human reason, but to human nature, of which reason is but a part and not the greatest part'. In his essay *On the Present Discontents* (1770), he explained that nations are not primarily ruled by laws, and even less by force. Rather, they are governed by a judicious management of 'the temper of the people'. However government is formally constituted, you will find that 'infinitely the greater part of it must depend upon the exercise of the powers that are left at large to the prudence and uprightness of ministers of state'. Without this temper, without these habits and customs, the 'commonwealth is no better than a scheme upon paper; and not a living, active, effective constitution'.

The 20th-century philosopher who did most to explain the constitutional implications of this was Michael Oakeshott. In *Rationalism in Politics* (1962), Oakeshott highlighted the superiority of the English approach, pointing to the deficiencies of the Rationalist mentality which underpins the modern constitutional concept. The Rationalist, he argued, is 'the enemy of authority, of prejudice, of the merely traditional, customary or habitual'. Nothing is of value merely because it exists; there is no opinion, custom, or belief that is not to be measured by the power of the Rationalist's reason. The cumulation of experience is registered only when rendered orderly, distinct, and converted to a formula. Politics becomes a type of engineering. The notion of founding a state upon a Declaration of the Rights of Man is a typical product of the Rationalist brain. But the error of Rationalism is that of discounting practical knowledge, knowledge acquired from usage and experience, believing only in scientific knowledge—the precise formulation in rules and principles of that which can be written down, taught, and learned.

Oakeshott's primary concern was how the Rationalist disposition had come to shape modern political practice, as measured by 'the extent to which traditions of behaviour have given place to ideologies, the extent to which the politics of destruction and creation have been substituted for the politics of repair, the consciously planned and deliberately executed being considered (for that reason) better than what has grown up and established itself unselfconsciously over a period of time'. His argument that politics, as a tradition of behaviour, was being replaced by doctrine and technique also has specific constitutional implications.

The American colonists—a society of 'self-made men'—took the analysis that Locke and others had distilled from the English political tradition and converted it into a set of doctrines based on abstract principles. The Declaration of Independence takes its place alongside the French Declaration of Rights as one of the sacred documents of Rationalist politics and also one of the founding texts of the modern concept of a constitution. In contrast, the English tradition exemplified in Magna Carta (1215), the Petition of Right (1628), or the Bill of Rights (1689) had been to declare and corroborate the old rather than make the new. But in these late 18th-century documents, universal principles rather than traditional practices were declared. Rights that had been the fruits of custom and practice were transplanted into the new world, where they were declared to be the product of 'nature'. What was exported as 'the concrete rights of an Englishman', Oakeshott argued, 'have returned home as the abstract Rights of Man, and they have returned to confound our politics and corrupt our minds'. He was contending that modern constitutions are not codifications produced as a consequence of modern circumstances. They are the products of a Rationalism that has distorted the legacy of the evolutionary British constitution.

The spirit informing the British constitution is exemplified in the English legal tradition. This is rooted in the practices of the English common law, a body of ancient custom—a set of usages, practices, and rulings that have evolved from time immemorial. The common law is 'unwritten law', with judicial authority limited to what it actually decides; it does not even establish law for a proposition that may seem to follow logically from it. As Chief Justice Coke was obliged to inform James I at the beginning of the 17th century, the common law is a type of 'artificial reason' and it 'requires long study and experience before that a man can attain to the cognizance of it'. Its nature is revealed in the practices of the bar, where competence is acquired not by scholastic education but by apprenticeship to a pupil master, during which the pupil learns the techniques of drafting and pleading, acquiring the sort of practical knowledge that can be distilled only from experienced advocacy. And this tradition is bolstered by the profession of a cloistered judiciary, drawn from the ranks of senior barristers and

Box 1: The method of common law

Lord Halsbury, Quinn v Leatham [1901] AC 495, 506: 'A case is only an authority for what it actually decides. I entirely deny that it can be quoted for a proposition that may seem to follow logically from it. Such a mode of reasoning assumes that the law is necessarily a logical code, whereas every lawyer must acknowledge that the law is not always logical at all.'

working not from general principle but from precedent to precedent (see Box 1).

In a sense, the British constitution is an extension of the methods of the common law to the activity of governing; unwritten law mutates into the idea of the unwritten constitution. If we try to convert the traditional British constitution into something analogous to the modern concept—that is, to treat it as a set of rules establishing and regulating the activity of governing—the constitution may seem random. It is revealed as a miscellaneous collection of statutes, rules, and guidelines, none of which constitutes 'higher law' and many of which make little sense until they are interpreted in the light of innumerable political understandings. The British constitution is, at heart, an assemblage of customary practices, with the 'rules' often amounting to no more than cribs distilled from such practices. This is a traditional constitution, an inheritance, a partnership between past, present, and future.

There are a number of key questions that this chapter highlights and which will be taken up in the chapters that follow:

- In the light of Britain's peculiar heritage, how have scholars dealt with the challenge of writing about the 'unwritten constitution'? Presenting a clear account of the workings of a traditional, customary, evolutionary constitution is some task, not least because a constitution that thrives on ambiguity and informality is one in which political and constitutional questions are constantly intertwined. This question is addressed in Chapter 2.

- What are the constitutional practices that give the British constitution its distinctive character? This is answered in Chapter 3, where it is explained that these practices are primarily those that shape the British tradition of parliamentary government.

- How does the traditional constitution change, first when the English state is transformed into the British state and thereafter as it acquires an extensive empire? More recently, to what extent are constitutional questions relevant to the loss of empire, to the reconfiguration of the governing arrangements of the several nations of the United Kingdom, and to integration of the UK with the European Union? The consequences of these complicated territorial changes are addressed in Chapter 4.

- The great virtue of the 'matchless constitution' was its ability to reconcile order and liberty: the British constitution aspired to be the 'constitution of liberty'. How is civil liberty protected in the British system? How is it maintained in the face of pressures arising from the extension of administrative government? These issues are addressed in Chapter 5.

- What remains of the traditional constitution? The concluding chapter brings together the primary concerns of the preceding chapters: the incipient Rationalism of writtenness, the waning of parliamentary authority, the loss of identity inherent in changing territorial forms of the state, the whittling away of civil liberty. It asks whether Rationalism is now the driving feature in contemporary government and whether the time has finally come when, in order to protect traditional constitutional values, a modern entrenched British constitution is needed.

Chapter 2
Writing the constitution

> The wiser and more public-spirited a nation is, and the more
> excellent its constitution, the fewer written constitutional
> laws it has, for these laws are only props, and a building has
> no need of props except when it has slipped out of vertical or
> been violently shaken by some external force.
>
> Joseph de Maistre, *Study on Sovereignty*, 1795.

Authority and liberty

Regarding their constitution as the inheritance of a long tradition
in the practical art of governing, the British have always been
reluctant to commit its basic rules to writing. Such reticence is
understandable: if constitutional understanding is acquired
through experience, the type of knowledge it embodies cannot
easily be expressed in books or conveyed through formal
instruction. Since formal rules are not the source of constitutional
behaviour, any attempt to codify the constitution will change it.
British government does, of course, operate in accordance with
rules, but rules of procedure and precedent rather than of
principle.

Throughout the 18th and 19th centuries, writers extolled the
virtues of the British constitution without being at all clear about
the way it worked. For those of a scientific temperament, this

could be most frustrating. Yet a certain group of scholars—those coming from abroad—became very interested in unlocking the secret of the constitution, not least because they were intrigued to understand how the British had managed to make the transition to modernity without undergoing violent revolution. The works of such distinguished European jurists as Montesquieu, de Lolme, von Gneist, and Redlich provide some of the most penetrating insights into the nature of the British constitution, even when revealing as much about their own political concerns as about the actualities of British governing practices. Many readers come away from their studies confirmed in the view that the constitution rests on some ineffable genius of the British in political matters.

To the extent that the British themselves wrote about their constitution, these were mainly works of history. Two antagonistic themes run through these histories: *authority*, especially the hierarchically imposed order of monarchical rule, and *liberty*, the free delegation of governmental authority from below, expressing a democratic sentiment. The concept of 'mixed government' extolled in the 'matchless constitution' is one expression of their reconciliation. More often these two themes are in direct conflict, with constitutional development driven by the struggle between them. The longest-standing expression of this conflict occurs in accounts of the feudal order and the ancient constitution or, more lyrically, between the Norman Yoke and the Gothic Bequest.

The Norman Yoke and the Gothic Bequest

The controversy between feudal order and ancient constitution takes us directly to the significance of the Conquest of 1066. There seems little doubt today that this was indeed a conquest: following successful military invasion, William of Normandy declared the entire land of England to be royal property and, after retaining almost 20 per cent himself, he proceeded to reward his chief vassals with estates amounting to around 40 per cent of the land.

The Normans asserted their sovereign power with a monarchical display of top-down authority, imposing a hierarchy of feudal law on the English.

Such an account was vigorously contested during the early 17th century by Sir Edward Coke, Chief Justice of the King's Bench and later a leading parliamentarian. In his influential work *Institutes of the Laws of England* (1628–44), Coke conferred judicial authority on the doctrine of the ancient constitution and the immemorial common law. He argued that the common law, a body of unchanging custom, existed 'time out of the mind of man' and pre-dated the Normans. Coke maintained that William had vindicated his claim to England in trial by battle and took the throne of England subject to those ancient laws. Coke's claim was that the common law was Anglo-Saxon in origin. It constituted a body of fundamental law that bound both kings and subjects.

This was just one strand of a broader political argument circulating during the 17th century: that ancient English liberties were a bequest from the early Saxons, or Goths as they were then called. The governing arrangements of the Goths, the argument ran, amounted to an ancient, pre-feudal, and law-observing constitution that preserved liberty. At the core of the arrangements was the great meeting, the *Witenagemote*, where freeborn Anglo-Saxons met to make law and deliberate over the great affairs of the kingdom. As Montesquieu later put it: 'the English have taken their idea of political government from the Germans. This fine system was found in the forests.'

The claim that the English possessed an ancient Gothic constitution has been widely used for political purposes. Arguing that 1066 marked no decisive break in legal continuity, advocates of the Gothic constitution rejected the Norman claim of absolute sovereign power: kings of England, including William I, occupied an office of limited authority and ruled according to the ancient fundamental laws of the land. The Gothic argument also challenges the standard historical account that Parliament came into existence only in the latter half of the 13th century as an instrument of Norman policy. It was claimed instead that the rights of the Commons derive from the ancient *Witenagemote*: the rights of 'freeborn Englishmen' to meet in Parliament derived directly from the ancient constitution, independent of sanction by kings.

This narrative about the ancient constitution spawned a related notion of the Norman Yoke. By imposing an alien feudalism on the pre-existing liberty-preserving structure of English government, the Normans corrupted the purity of the original Anglo-Saxon constitution. This claim gave rise to a peculiar form of constitutional reasoning: that all political struggles for liberty were really appeals for the restoration of ancient, immemorial liberties. So the great constitutional documents of Magna Carta (1215), the Petition of Right (1628), and the Bill of Rights (1689) did not enact anything new. 'In all our great political struggles', proclaimed the 19th-century constitutional historian E. A. Freeman, 'the voice of the Englishman has never called for the assertion of new principles, for the enactment of new laws; the cry has always been for the better observance of the laws which were already in force, for the redress of grievances which had arisen from their corruption or neglect.' English constitutional development, it was asserted, is marked by the degree to which, through political struggle, these ancient liberties—real or imagined—have been restored.

During the 17th-century conflicts, these competing narratives formed part of the ideological weaponry of both royalist and parliamentary forces. Stuart kings loudly proclaimed the absolute nature of their prerogative powers to rule the kingdom; the absolute prerogative of the crown, wrote James I, 'is no subject for the tongue of a lawyer'. Parliamentary lobbies, by contrast, drew on the idea of the Gothic bequest to argue that the true source of governmental power lay with 'the people', which meant their representatives in Parliament. With royalists maintaining that Parliament was convened and dissolved purely according to the king's will and parliamentarians claiming that the Commons alone was the repository of all governmental authority, the conflict was strained to breaking point. Failure to resolve this dispute through political accommodation led directly to the dramatic events of the mid-century: civil war, defeat of the royalist cause, execution of the king, formation of the Commonwealth and Protectorate, and then, in 1660, restoration of the monarchy.

These events had a major impact on the shape of the modern British constitution. The modern constitution came into being after the Revolution of 1688 when, once James II had fled the kingdom, a convention Parliament—formed without any king to convene it—offered the throne to William and Mary on terms laid down in the Bill of Rights. The legacy is ambivalent. The upheavals had been literally revolutionary, in the sense of having gone round full circle and back to a monarchical arrangement. But because of this complete rotation, the legitimizing principles of modern constitutional government became ambiguous. Was the king above the three estates of lords, bishops, and commons as the law of the constitution stated? Should the king be treated as one of three equal component parts of the sovereign Parliament (king, lords, and commons) as the emerging doctrine of parliamentary sovereignty implied? Should the commons, as sole representative voice of the people, now be accorded clear primacy in the constitution, as the emerging principle of popular sovereignty suggested? These were the questions that had to be fudged both to maintain the stability of the post-1688 state and to strengthen the authority of its governing institutions. The modern settlement was marked from the outset by a singular reluctance to avoid any close examination of its founding principles.

This characteristic of post-1688 constitutional writing helped to shape a distinctively English style of constitutional scholarship, later called the Whig interpretation of history. The great

19th-century Whig historians conceived the English constitution as an elaborate cultural heritage whose study provided a boundless source of prescriptive wisdom. It was the story of the triumph of liberty over absolute sovereign power, evidenced by the increasing importance of representative institutions in the British system. One central theme was the need for nuance and for the maintenance of ambiguity, which manifested itself in distaste for the infelicities of the lawyerly approach to the subject.

Constitutional history, they complained, had been perverted by lawyers. This was because 'the legal mind' is congenitally unable to grasp ambiguity, uncertainty, or heterogeneity and is therefore incapable of sensitive historical understanding. This intellectual defect was linked to a political deficiency. The natural tendency of the legal mind, they suggested, is conservative: it constantly defers to authority. A lack of mental subtlety together with a conservative temperament rendered the lawyer's account of the constitution deficient. The entire concept of sovereignty, they complained, was a lawyer's invention, nowhere to be found in the historical records. And the main culprit was the 18th-century lawyer Sir William Blackstone.

Blackstone's *Commentaries*

Appointed to the newly established chair in English Law at Oxford, Blackstone in his *Commentaries on the Laws of England* (1765–9) wrote the first modern account of the laws of England. Its publication was a runaway success, not only in England but throughout the Empire and especially in British North America, where it provided lawyers and judges with an authoritative text in lieu of the practical experience acquired at the Inns of Court in London. Blackstone wrote the work specifically to educate 'the guardians of the English constitution; the makers, repealers, and interpreters of the English laws'. He certainly succeeded: the *Commentaries* became the most influential 18th-century account of British constitutional law.

The *Commentaries* spearheaded the movement for teaching the basic principles of common law, as distinct from canon law and Roman law, as part of university study. It presented the entire body of English law as a system of national law. Since it was commonly believed that the main supporters of royal absolutism were civil lawyers (scholars of Roman law), this initiative enhanced the scholarly status of the indigenous liberty-protecting common law. Blackstone argued that the common law was uniquely English and superior to all other types of law. The *Commentaries* did much to bolster the emerging ideology of nationalism.

Blackstone viewed English constitutional history in the conventional terms of Whig history as the 'gradual restoration of that ancient constitution whereof our Saxon forefathers had been unjustly deprived, partly by the policy and partly by the force, of the Norman'. But—and this is where he parted company with Whig historians—he also saw the necessity for an absolute central power.

Recognizing that the king's prerogative powers were subject to law, Blackstone acknowledged that most of these powers had been retained in the law of the constitution after 1688. And in the manner of their exercise, the king was given very wide latitude. Being 'out of the ordinary course of the common law', these prerogative powers were special and must be treated delicately and deferentially. This was so because the law of the constitution, as distinct from its practice, still 'ascribes to the king, in his high political character ... attributes of a great and transcendent nature'. In law, the king was not simply the chief but the sole magistrate of the nation, since all other government officials acted by virtue of his commission. No court could have jurisdiction over the king.

But Blackstone skirted round constitutional fundamentals. He noted, for example, that 17th-century convention parliaments had met without the authority of the king, but explained that they were established of necessity, their actions subsequently being authorized by the king. And whenever faced with politically contentious issues he invariably retreated to formal legal analysis. Maintaining that the basic legal principle of the constitution was that of the sovereign authority of parliament, he explained that here 'parliament' did not mean the people's representatives in the Commons. It was a purely legal concept, the king convening the three estates of the realm. This is the Crown-in-Parliament: far from being an expression of democratic or popular sentiment, it is a formal expression of state sovereignty.

Blackstone emphasized that the jurisdiction of the Crown-in-Parliament is absolute. This was the institution in which 'that absolute despotic power, which must in all governments reside somewhere, is entrusted by the constitution of these kingdoms'. Its power knew no limits:

> It can regulate or new model the succession to the crown; as was done in the reign of Henry VIII and William III. It can alter the established religion of the land; as was done in a variety of instances, in the reigns of king Henry VIII and his three children. It can change and create afresh *even the constitution of the kingdom* and of parliaments themselves; as was done by the act of union, and the several statutes for triennial and septennial elections. It can, in short, do everything that is not naturally impossible.

Since there were no limitations on the authority of this institution, the fundamental rule of the constitution could be reduced to a single sentence: what the Crown-in-Parliament enacts is law.

In this juristic analysis, Blackstone downplayed the checks and balances of the three components of Parliament in favour of the conceptual unity of the Crown-in-Parliament. Rather than extolling the authority of the common law as immemorial custom—and therefore as 'fundamental law'—he presented law as a simple positive entity: the commands of the Crown-in-Parliament.

Dicey on the *Law of the Constitution*

During the late 18th and early 19th centuries, Jeremy Bentham and his utilitarian disciples engaged in a sustained attempt at removing what they believed were the taints of Toryism, Anglicanism, and natural law permeating Blackstone's account of the constitution. The most influential outcome of this movement was A. V. Dicey's *Lectures on the Law of the Constitution* first published in 1885. Dicey, successor to Blackstone at Oxford, was the first to examine the British constitution using an analytical legal method.

Dicey's account began by both criticizing the formalism of Blackstone and castigating those who extol the virtues of the ancient Gothic constitution and promote the Whig interpretation of history. For Dicey, the former provided a skewed version of constitutional law, while the latter amounted either to 'simple antiquarianism' or offered an 'astounding method', treating 'every step towards civilisation' as 'a step backwards towards the simple wisdom of our uncultured ancestors'. Dicey's stated aim was to rescue the constitution from the historians' grasp and to lay bare its legal fundamentals.

An exponent of analytical legal positivism, Dicey believed that the duty of an English professor of law was 'to state what are the laws which form part of the constitution, to arrange them in their order, to explain their meaning, and to exhibit where possible their logical connection'. Constitutional law was concisely defined as 'all rules which directly or indirectly affect the distribution or the exercise of the sovereign power of the state'. These were the rules which defined the members of the sovereign power, regulated their relations, and determined the mode through which sovereign power exercised its authority. The most significant word in his definition was 'rules'. Dicey used that term rather than 'laws' and divided rules into two types: laws in the strict sense, enforced by the courts, and conventions defined as 'understandings, habits or practices' which, though they regulate the conduct of members of the sovereign power, are not enforceable in courts.

With this simple and elegant approach, Dicey was able to convert the British constitution into an assemblage of rules. His method placed the constitutional lawyer at the centre of constitutional scholarship: rather than simply venerating the constitution, lawyers must analyse its basic precepts and search for 'the guidance of first principles'.

Dicey identified three guiding principles of the British constitution: the legislative sovereignty of the Crown-in-Parliament, the universal rule throughout the constitution of ordinary law (the 'rule of law'), and the role which constitutional conventions play in the ordering of the constitution. His objective in the *Law of the Constitution* was to explain these principles and demonstrate their interdependence.

Dicey defined the principle of legislative sovereignty both positively and negatively. It meant that 'under the English constitution' the Crown-in-Parliament had 'the right to make or unmake any law whatsoever'. There could be no limitation on legislative competence and no special laws—such as constitutional laws—protected from repeal or amendment. It followed that 'no person or body is recognised...as having the right to override or set aside the legislation of Parliament'. The primary duty of the judiciary was to give full and faithful effect to the laws enacted in legislation; judges were the precision instruments of legislation. He expressed no interest in what he called 'speculative difficulties' presented by trying to identify possible limits to this power; he simply followed Blackstone in claiming that supreme legislative authority 'must exist in every civilised state'.

Dicey's first principle is a principle of *authority*. But he argued that it meshes with the second principle of the constitution—that of the rule of law—to promote *liberty*. Parliamentary sovereignty promoted the 'supremacy of law' because Parliament's commands 'can be uttered only through the combined actions of its three constituent parts', creating a rigid legality that restricts the actions of the executive. For Dicey, the 'rule of law' meant primarily the 'absolute supremacy...of regular law as opposed to the influence of arbitrary power'. This rests on the principle of equality before the law, of 'the equal subjection of all classes to the ordinary law of the land administered by the ordinary Law Courts'. In practice, the rigid legality implicit in the traditions of the common law bolstered the principle of the rule of law.

But these two guiding constitutional principles did not exist in harmony. Assume, for example, that Parliament enacts a statute that states: 'The Secretary of State may make an order to hold any person whose detention appears to him to be expedient in the interests of the public safety or security of the realm.' If you are dragged from your bed in the middle of the night by police officers enforcing a properly drafted order and then detained for an indefinite period without any explanation other than the Minister's word, you might feel that, even if this executive action is valid according to the principle of legislative sovereignty, it can scarcely be said to comply with the principle of the rule of law. How can these two principles be reconciled?

The answer, Dicey suggested, is found in the third guiding principle: the role performed by constitutional conventions. Harmony between the first two principles came about through the working practices of the British constitution. These practices— precepts of political morality which Dicey calls 'constitutional conventions'—ensured that the laws of the constitution, including the crown's prerogative powers, were exercised in accordance with a spirit of liberty. These conventional rules regulate the constituent parts of Parliament, ensuring the accountability of the executive to Parliament, and of Parliament to the public. Dicey's account of the law of the constitution rested on a delicate set of balances operating within these parliamentary mechanisms.

Bagehot on *The English Constitution*

If Dicey founded the scholarly discipline of British constitutional law, then Walter Bagehot provided the basis for the political scientist's account of the British constitution. In *The English Constitution* (1867), Bagehot sought to rescue the constitution from the hands of lawyers by challenging two erroneous interpretations. The first was the separation of powers, a doctrine propounded by Montesquieu with respect to the British constitution and which Blackstone had plagiarized. The second was the idea that British government operated through some Diceyan balance between monarchy, aristocracy, and commons.

Central to Bagehot's method is the distinction between the 'dignified' and the 'efficient' versions of the constitution. The dignified version focuses on the ancient, complex, and ceremonial aspects of the constitution. These 'excite and preserve the reverence of the population' and thereby generate 'its motive power'. The efficient version focuses on the modern, simple, and functional aspects. These deploy that power; they are the parts 'by which it, in fact, works and rules'.

Bagehot's distinction explained how a modern system of government was able to evolve within the shell of the ancient constitution. The dignified version, 'august with the Gothic grandeur of a more imposing age', exerted its 'imaginative attraction upon an uncultured and rude population' while permitting the sophisticated practices of party politics and parliamentary government to emerge in its shadows. An ancient constitution, he observed, is 'like an old man who still wears with attached fondness clothes in the fashion of his youth: what you see of him is the same; what you do not see is wholly altered'. In this way, the British state maintained the outer trappings of a monarchy, while becoming in reality a 'disguised republic'.

The symbolism of the queen, Bagehot contended, was incalculable. The monarch offered a visible symbol of unity and strengthened government with the power of religion. The greatest function of monarchy was to disguise, shrouding in mystery the real workings of modern government. Only by maintaining this façade could the idea of a separation of powers between the queen's government, the Parliament, and the judiciary be preserved or the imagery of balance between monarchy, aristocracy, and commons retained. Far from being based on separation, in fact the constitution worked because of 'the close union, the nearly complete fusion of the executive and legislative powers'. This was the 'efficient secret' of the constitution. At its core was the institution of the Cabinet, a committee unknown to law but which, being 'a committee of the legislative body selected to be the executive body', was the most powerful institution in the British system.

Bagehot's book warned against any account of the British constitution that separates law from practice, forms from the actuality. The queen may be the head of the constitution in its dignified version, but the Prime Minister rules according to the efficient. The queen may be, in Blackstone's words, 'the fountain of honour', but the Treasury is 'the spring of business'. The crown maintained a symbol of unity, but the system of government works only through disciplined party division. The forms suggest separation, but the practice reveals layers of connections.

Bagehot was the last of the great Whig writers. His classic work, written on the eve of the second Reform Act, expressed mid-Victorian anxieties about the coming of democracy. He believed the country would be unable to make the transition to democracy without maintaining a 'theatrical show' inspiring deference amongst the multitude and bolstering the aristocratic character of the traditional constitution. He was not optimistic. The coming of democracy in England might not lead, as in France, to the guillotine, but he predicted it would lead to the rule of money, especially of 'new money working upon ignorance for its own ends'. Democracy would not come about by sudden revolution but it would just as surely impair the constitution, and it would do this by 'spoiling our Parliament'.

Twentieth-century constitutional writing

Before the 20th century, constitutional commentary was written exclusively for the edification of the governing class. The proper functioning of the Victorian constitution depended on what Bagehot called the 'upper ten thousand', those 'persons and families possessed of equal culture, and equal faculties, and equal spirit'. This functioning was enhanced by education in a common tradition of conduct, which is why Gladstone believed that 'the public schools of England are part of the constitution'. Bagehot called this arrangement one of 'club government'. Government by a club, he declared, is a 'standing wonder', resting on the high degree of trust in those who exercise power. It worked because all public officials—Ministers, parliamentarians, judges, and civil servants—had internalized a common, though implicit, code of conduct.

During the 20th century, things changed. The most profound change was the arrival of democracy, with universal adult suffrage finally being achieved in 1928. Democracy brought the Labour party to prominence as parliamentary representatives of the working class, swiftly replacing the Liberals in the two-party system organized around Government and Opposition. Representative democracy produced important changes in political behaviour, signalled by the institutionalization of ideological politics—the politics of programme, manifesto, and rule book, whether based on Bentham, Marx, or Hayek—and by the emergence of party discipline as a key determinant of political conduct. It also led to unprecedented growth in the powers of government, with government assuming responsibility both for the management of the economy and the welfare of citizens.

Yet these dramatic shifts in government and politics generated little constitutional debate. Warnings were periodically issued about the dangers posed by unchecked growth in the administrative powers of government, most stridently in Chief

Justice Hewart's contention in 1929 that Britain was on the brink of a 'new despotism'. But given the nature of the constitution, it was difficult to disentangle constitutional threats from political disputes. In addition, political parties were more interested in winning elections than debating constitutional questions. The problem for the Conservatives was that Dicey's principle of the rule of law—especially its incompatibility with the existence of executive discretionary powers—was patently unrealistic, and Conservatives were nothing if not realistic. The challenge facing Labour, by contrast, was not to reform the constitution but to transform society, and the powers bequeathed to government in Bagehot's efficient version of the constitution seemed well suited to the task.

As a result, until the closing decades of the 20th century there was a remarkable dearth of writing about the constitution. Dicey's conservative assumptions in the *Law of the Constitution* had been challenged from the left by Ivor Jennings's *Law and the Constitution* (1933), but both recognized—notwithstanding their varying use of conjunctions—that *constitution* and *law* were distinct entities. Lawyers began to feel more comfortable in writing about 'constitutional law', but since this was not a technical term of English law its usage was largely a matter of convenience and taste. Without an authoritative legal framework, constitutional lawyers were drawn to descriptive and analytical studies of the principal institutions of government, exemplified in the work of Jennings himself, with his books on *Cabinet Government* (1936), *Parliament* (1939), and *Local Government in the Modern Constitution* (1933). This working method reinforced the conviction that the constitution was merely an object of description, illustrated by Jennings's observation in 1936 that 'the British constitution is changing so rapidly that it is difficult to keep pace with it'. We certainly find nothing in legal scholarship analogous to the normative frameworks of constitutional treatises written by jurists working in regimes with modern constitutions.

Interestingly, this type of institutional analysis did not change with the establishment in the post-war period of university politics departments. Even more than lawyers, political scientists concentrated on studying the institutions of government to the neglect of constitutional reflection. Knowledge of the British system of government was enhanced by studies of the Cabinet, central and local government, national industries, Parliament, and political parties. But their concern was with efficiency and effectiveness rather than constitutional propriety. In *The British Cabinet* (1962), J. P. Mackintosh criticized the tendency to confer authority on a certain pattern of British government 'based on a simplified version of what did take place in the last third of the nineteenth century'. In reality, 'all of our institutions change as British society and world conditions alter'. It wasn't surprising, therefore, that in the following year John Griffith quipped that 'the constitution is what happens'.

From the mid-1970s, however, the tone began to change. Concerns about economic decline and government overload caused political scientists to engage in more critical examination of the effectiveness of the British system of government. Reflections on 'the state of the nation' caused some to speculate that perhaps the difficulties were not only economic and political: they might also be constitutional. An early illustration is Nevil Johnson's *In Search of the Constitution* (1977) which promoted the thesis that the constitutional dimension to the British disease manifested itself in 'the atrophy of any language in which we can talk of constitutional issues, of rules, or of principles of public law'. Arguing that the traditional language of the British constitution had lost its vitality and ability to sustain authority, Johnson contended that 'we are left floundering in a world of pure pragmatism'. Bagehot might have correctly distinguished between dignified and efficient versions of the constitution but in his concern to describe reality he saw the constitution solely as a mechanism and ignored the task of exposing its operative values and principles. Johnson concluded that Bagehot's offspring had continued to treat the constitution in such terms, thereby hampering the possibility of constitutional renewal.

From the 1980s onwards, these ideas were established as a new orthodoxy. It has today become almost impossible to write about the British constitution without explicitly advocating the need for reform. From a variety of perspectives, scholars and publicists have written extensively over the last twenty or so years to demonstrate that with respect to constitutional matters the British have lost their way. In some accounts—such as David Marquand's *The Unprincipled Society* (1988) and Will Hutton's *The State We're In* (1995)—deficiencies in Britain's constitutional arrangements form a central part of a wider theme: that Britain's economic decline is the product of its inability to adapt to modernity. Constitutional renewal has become the precondition for economic regeneration.

Codifying conventions

One strand of this new orthodoxy is the call to codify the constitution. So far, this proposal has made no political headway. When Labour was elected in 1997, it was committed to a major programme of 'constitutional modernization', yet it displayed no interest in producing a systematic codification of the existing constitutional rules. Although it introduced major reforms— including devolution, reform of the House of Lords, freedom of information, and the Human Rights Act—it created no new constitutional settlement. Vernon Bogdanor's recent book *The New Constitution* (2009) argues that these reforms have resulted in the demise of the old constitution and the creation of a new one. His book claims to do for the post-1997 arrangements what Dicey and Bagehot did for the Victorian constitution. But whatever the analytical merits of Bogdanor's work, it sketches a 'new constitution' only in Jennings's sense that some things have changed.

But something new has occurred in the last twenty years. This is the widespread conviction that the so-called unwritten rules of constitutional practice must now be formalized. There have always been moments in history when it has been politic to formulate a conventional understanding in parliamentary statute: the restrictions on prerogative powers in the Bill of Rights of 1689, the position of the House of Lords with respect to money Bills in the Parliament Act 1911, the relationship between Parliament and the Dominions in the Statute of Westminster 1931 are illustrations. But these were taken as signs of progressive evolutionary change in governing arrangements. The current move to formalize is different. It signals the fact that, despite embodying important values, the conventions seem no longer to carry adequate authority: they must now be beefed up in written, codified form.

This can be illustrated with reference to the Cabinet Paper *Questions of Procedure for Ministers*, first issued by Prime Minister Attlee in 1945. This confidential document laid down general guidelines of ministerial conduct distilled from precedents of previous administations. Reproduced with amendments for all post-war governments, the document was declassified only in 1992. Beginning as 'tips on etiquette' it has evolved into a more elaborate code of conduct for Ministers covering potential conflicts between public duties and private interests, ministerial and parliamentary responsibilities, and governmental and party roles. It is now produced by the Cabinet Office as the *Ministerial Code*. That document was complemented in 1996 by the publication of a *Civil Service Code* that specified core values of integrity, honesty, objectivity, and impartiality. And in the Constitutional Reform and Governance Act 2010, these values, together with management arrangements for the civil service, were placed on a statutory foundation.

This process of formalization has its origins in a general sense of decline in political conduct, exemplified by the scandal in the 1990s involving MPs accepting cash for asking parliamentary questions. The resulting crisis led to the establishment of the Committee on Standards in Public Life. In addition to recommending the adoption of the above codes, the committee also proposed the formulation of a new Code of Conduct for MPs overseen by an Independent Parliamentary Commissioner for Standards, an arrangement introduced in 1995. Then, in 2009, in the wake of the MPs' expenses scandal, the ability of MPs to set their own expenses regime was removed and transferred to a new Independent Parliamentary Standards Authority, which is given authority by statute to draft and police the new rules. Most recently, the government in October 2011 published the *Cabinet Manual*, a 110-page document that provides 'a source of information on the laws, conventions and rules that affect the operation and procedures of the Government'.

These recent reforms have laid down an elaborate regime of formal rules concerning ministerial, MP, and civil servant conduct. Cumulatively, they have driven a cart and horses through the informal, trust-based arrangements of club government. But the process of converting the informal practices of British government into formal rules to be policed by newly established independent agencies does not signal the emergence of a new constitution. It merely marks the extent to which the old constitution has lost its guiding spirit and must now be shored up by formal rules. The old is dead; the new is yet to be born.

Chapter 3
Parliamentary government

England is governed not by logic but by Parliament.

Benjamin Disraeli, 1871.

Parliament: the mirror of the nation

The most distinctive feature of the British constitution is found in its arrangements for parliamentary government. That Britain made an evolutionary, not revolutionary, transition to modernity is attributable in large part to the flexibility of those practices. But parliamentary government is misunderstood if, as often happens today, these practices are made to fit a template of modern constitutionalism and Parliament's role is limited to that of a legislature. The peculiar strength of parliamentary government lies in the complexity and ambiguity of its institutional arrangements and in the confluence rather than separation of governing tasks.

Tasks assumed by Parliament have varied considerably. At times an opposition to the overweening power of government, Parliament has also been deployed as a powerful instrument of government. Often portrayed as a beacon of liberal democracy, Parliament has at critical moments been the tool of both monarchy and oligarchy. Presenting itself as a legislature, Parliament has also undertaken important roles as a council and a court. Since its formation in the late 13th century, Parliament has continued to exist, enduring many upheavals in government. And its survival owes as much to its weakness and mutability as to its strength.

The simple fact of its continued existence is the single most important indicator of the character of Britain's evolutionary constitutional arrangements. Parliament became the primary means through which the English forged both a sense of political unity and a national identity. To an extent unusual in European practices of governing, the English Parliament came to symbolize the 'political nation'. The central place assumed by Parliament in governing arrangements is the main reason why the British have never devised a legal concept of the state. It is also the main reason why a system of administrative law was never established. And it is one of the main reasons why we have never developed a modern constitution. Parliament is the key to understanding the peculiar character of both the British constitution and the British state.

The main objectives of this chapter are to explain how Parliament came to assume this central place as the 'mirror of the nation', to assess its role today, and to consider what implications its role has for understanding the current state of the British constitution. In essence, practices of parliamentary government are products of a rich history of struggle between the crown and the communities of the realm, with the crown holding on to its prerogatives of governing against those who, in the name of liberty, sought to limit those powers and place them in fixed institutional forms. This struggle led eventually to the emergence of a distinctive composite sovereign authority, that of the Crown-in-Parliament. But this was achieved only after civil war (1642–9), the execution of Charles I (1649), the formation of the Commonwealth and Protectorate (1649–60), the restoration of the king (1660), and a revolution which led to the removal of James II and, at the instigation of a convention Parliament, the installation on the throne of William and Mary (1688). Only after the Revolution of 1688 did the conditions exist for the emergence of what Dicey identified as the twin features of the constitution: the concept of parliamentary sovereignty and the principle of government by law.

Origins of Parliament

Parliament's origins lie in late 13th-century political developments. The Norman Conquest quickly led to the creation of a unified and highly centralized kingdom which ensured that the political feudalism characteristic of many European kingdoms—in which the king had to negotiate with powerful barons—did not evolve. A strong monarchy was established in England, but the danger was that this monarchical power would be abused.

This threat materialized in the late 12th century as the Angevin kings sought to use their powerbase in England to expand their continental empire. After a series of disastrous wars in which King John lost Normandy in 1204 and suffered defeats in Flanders and France in 1214, the barons struck back. Their aim was to challenge the system of Norman government that had been constructed over the previous 150 years by requiring the king to grant a charter of liberties. This was the Magna Carta of 1215.

Magna Carta was not some great work of the 'nation' or the 'people', as the Whig constitutional historians were later to claim. The barons asserted their authority primarily by requiring the king to govern through the council. By establishing the principle that acts of the king had an official character exercisable through certain forms, the Charter constituted a landmark in the emergence of English governing arrangements. Subsequent history is messy, with no consistent differentiation being achieved in law between the king and the crown, but it is from this concept of the crown—the king in his official capacity—that our understanding of government has evolved. The great significance of Magna Carta—in contrast to similar charters negotiated throughout continental Europe during this period—is that whereas the demand for liberties on the Continent led to barons obtaining independence within their fiefdoms, the objective of the English barons had been to acquire a share in an already well-established centralized and monarchical system of government.

One important provision of Magna Carta was the requirement that no taxes be levied 'except by the common counsel of our realm'. During the reign of Henry III (1216–72), the meeting of king and council was the form through which the 'community of the realm' expressed its will. But by the mid-13th century Henry had started to require each of the shires to send two knights to supplement the work of the council. This was the precedent for the formation of Parliament.

Parliament was consolidated during the 14th century as it became convenient to amalgamate the *estates*, the meeting with tenants-in-chief to discuss financial necessities, with *parlement*, the hearing of petitions in cases referred by the king's judges. It is in this latter sense that we trace Parliament's origins back to a high court. But only at the end of Edward III's long reign

1. 'You can read, right?—I want you to check this thing for loopholes'

(1327–77) was Parliament transformed from an event into an institution. The impetus that drove this was financial necessity: the need for revenues to meet the cost of the wars in France and Scotland.

The institution forged during this period acquired its strength from three sources. First, Parliament was formed from the union between a high court of justice and a body (the estates) charged with taxing and representative responsibilities. Once it was recognized that individual petitions contained common grievances, Parliament's role shifted from that of court to a more general governmental forum. Secondly, Parliament was a forum in which the council, the coordinating agent of the king's government, controlled the agenda. If Parliament had been formed simply as a body that checked the crown, it would have withered; its survival depended on its usefulness as an instrument of royal government. Thirdly, its mode of representation, which required attendance not just from the barons but also two representatives from each of the shires, ensured that the decisions of the 'knights of the shires' bound their constituents. Representation was not experienced as an expression of some democratic sentiment: it was seen as an incident of feudal service which was binding on local communities.

The English Parliament that evolved during the later Middle Ages originally came into being as an act of royal will. To claim continuity with the Anglo-Saxon *Witenagemote* thus seems rather strained. Often presented as an institution to counterbalance government, Parliament's origins lie essentially in its value in assisting the king in the business of governing. The great strength of this arrangement lay in the fact that the king's court, the king's council, and the king's Parliament together formed an elaborate system of multi-layered government. Integration rather than separation strengthened the structure. But there was an even more enduring legacy: the continued existence of Parliament ensured that a national system of government would be established on something deeper and broader than monarchical authority.

Parliament and the formation of the state

Parliamentary assemblies were a common feature of early 16th-century European regimes. Nevertheless, by the end of the century the English Parliament was one of few representative institutions still in existence. It owed its survival mainly to the use Henry VIII made of Parliament during the upheavals of the Reformation.

The great Reformation Parliament summoned by Henry in 1529 sat regularly and lasted for nearly seven years. Using the authority of the Crown-in-Parliament, Henry introduced statutes to eliminate medieval privileges which encumbered the exercise of his authority. Most of these belonged to the Church. The revolutionary act of breaking with the Church in Rome was one in which Henry made full use of the instrumentality of Parliament: crown and Parliament united to challenge rival jurisdictions. In a speech to Parliament in 1543, Henry maintained that 'we at no time stand so highly in our estate royal as in the time of Parliament; wherein we as head and you as members are conjoined and knit together into one body politic'. Parliament became a vital component of Tudor statecraft.

There was now no limitation on what the Crown-in-Parliament could determine. By legislative action, the Church was placed under the authority of the king and the established religion of the land was changed. These constitutional changes were here to stay. When Henry's offspring later sought to advance (Edward VI), reverse (Mary), or reintroduce the reforms (Elizabeth I) they could do so only by introducing new legislation in Parliament.

The Act of Parliament was now recognized as the highest expression of law. These actions enhanced in particular the authority of the House of Commons, which by the end of the 16th century had emerged as an independent body protective of its own privileges. When the Stuart kings tried to rule more informally, asserting their divine right, the stage was set for confrontation between the 'head' and the 'members' of this single 'body politic'.

Parliament initially responded to these informal methods of governing by reviving the power of impeachment. Since it was accepted that 'the king can do no wrong', any wrongfulness in government had to be attributed to the 'evil counsel' of his Ministers. Punishment for such evil counsel was enforced by the parliamentary procedure of impeachment. Impeachment actions against such leading Ministers as Sir Francis Bacon (1621), the Duke of Buckingham (1626–8), and the Earl of Strafford (1640–1) heightened the tensions between king and Parliament. They implied that the king was now merely a figurehead: by punishing the king's agents, Parliament was presuming to know what the public good required better than the king himself.

In 1629 Charles I's solution was to dissolve Parliament, ruling for the next eleven years without it. But he was forced to summon a Parliament in 1640, as he was desperate for additional revenue to raise an army against the rebellious Scots. At this point, Parliament acted decisively to set terms for the redress of grievances, laid down as Nineteen Propositions. The king's rejection of them on the grounds that they would lead to the destruction of the traditional 'mixed constitution' caused the country to drift into civil war. During this period, parliamentarians first began to state clearly that the true source of governmental power lay not in God, nor in the king as God's vicegerent on earth, but in the people. Under the English constitution that power was located in the Commons. Having come into existence as an act of royal will, Parliament—by invoking the principle of popular sovereignty— now assumed the power of self-creation.

Parliamentary forces eventually claimed victory in the civil war and Charles was placed on trial. His defence that 'the king can do no wrong' being rejected, he was found guilty of treason and in January 1649 was executed. England became a republic and the office of the king—along with the House of Lords and the established (Anglican) Church—was abolished. Parliament remained in existence as the formal locus of authority, but in reality power was held by the army. In 1653 the army effectively seized control, Oliver Cromwell was proclaimed Lord Protector, and the Instrument of Government—England's first and only written constitution—was drafted. But as the Puritan revolution unravelled, Parliament was dissolved in 1658 and then, after the death of Cromwell, in 1660 the monarchy—along with Parliament and the Church—was restored.

With the restoration of the monarchy under Charles II, son of the executed king, attempts were made to redefine the balance between the crown and Parliament, but many ambiguities remained. When in 1685 Charles was succeeded by his Catholic brother, James II sought to resolve these. His solution was to begin a programme of centralization and modernization modelled on the absolutist French regime of Louis XIV. But James's succession had divided the ruling elite: the Tories supported the principle of 'divine right', while the Whigs had wanted to exclude James from the throne on account of his Catholicism. When James proceeded to implement his policies and rule without Parliament, the Whig magnates, fearing a subversion of the constitution, sought help from the Protestant Dutch.

In November 1688, William of Orange—who was married to James's Protestant daughter Mary—landed in England at the head of an army. He pledged to uphold a free Parliament and was willing to negotiate terms enabling James to keep his throne, albeit with reduced powers. But in December James fled the country and the ruling elite determined that he had forfeited the crown. A convention Parliament was held and, in a compromise between adherence to the hereditary principle and 'reason of state' argument, invited William and Mary to reign jointly. This act established the principle that thereafter succession to the throne is determined by Act of Parliament.

The modern constitutional settlement

The terms of the constitutional settlement were formally expressed in the Bill of Rights of 1689. This Act affirmed the Protestant character of the English state and, by removing certain of the king's prerogatives, established a constitutional monarchy. More than this: by establishing the principle that prerogative powers could be abolished by Act of Parliament, the Bill of Rights led directly to the legal doctrine of Parliament's absolute legislative authority, underpinned by affirmation of the principle of free and regular Parliaments.

The 1688 Revolution placed the Whig magnates in a very powerful position, leading to a period—lasting almost eighty years—of Whig supremacy. In this period of relatively stable aristocratic rule, the main conventions of constitutional government were forged. It was also a period of great economic and social change during which Britain was transformed from an insular society with a largely agricultural economy to an industrial and commercial nation underpinned by a fiscal-military state of considerable imperial might. These developments are linked: constitutional modernization provided the conditions of political and commercial stability that fuelled the industrial revolution.

Constitutional conflicts of the 17th century had centred on the clash between the crown's divine right to rule and Parliament's claim to be the institution from which the king's government derived its powers. In adopting the composite form of Crown-in-Parliament as the source of authority, the 1689 settlement fudged the finer points of constitutional principle. Practical wisdom had decreed separation between government and legislature: although government remained in the hands of the king, Parliament possessed the ultimate instruments of control. The formal authority of the king's government was retained but it depended on an institution that presented itself as guardian of civil liberties. The 'matchless constitution' of parliamentary government survived not on the basis of fixed formal principles but on a procedural framework of considerable flexibility.

Consider, for example, the abiding 17th-century concern over standing armies which might be used as instruments of oppression. The Bill of Rights had declared such armies unlawful without the consent of Parliament, but this did not lead to their elimination. On the contrary, between 1680 and 1780 the British army and navy trebled in size. Command of military forces remained part of the crown's prerogative powers, but authority to sanction this growth rested with Parliament. The military thus became a tool of *national* rather than simply *royal* power. The post-1688 settlement did not lead to a reduction in the scale of government: it operated to ensure that Parliament would become a central player in the activity.

The settlement is generally labelled 'representative and responsible government'. Since the policies of the king's government had to be supported by Parliament, the most effective way of achieving this was to appoint parliamentary leaders as the king's Ministers. This led to renewed tensions as the crown used its powers of patronage to seduce leaders from allegiance to their parliamentary parties, and parliamentary parties in turn sought to acquire control over the government. It was a struggle that Parliament eventually won.

In the process, legal methods of ensuring governmental accountability were replaced by political methods. The legal procedure of impeachment fell into disuse when Parliament discovered a more informal but equally effective means of ensuring ministerial accountability: rather than pursuing formal legal proceedings, Parliament realized that a simple majority vote would suffice to require a Minister to resign. The legal principle that the king could do no wrong was retained only because the king eventually became a cipher, able to act only on the advice of others.

The process of establishing representative and responsible government was quickly consolidated as a result of complications over the royal succession. In the 1689 settlement it was assumed that once James II (in exile) and William III had died, the monarchy would revert to its normal course. This assumption foundered on the death of Anne's last surviving child in 1700: since Mary had died in 1694 and William and Mary had been childless the Protestant line would end with Anne (Mary's sister, who became queen in 1702). On hereditary lines, James II's son, Prince James Francis Edward Stuart ('the Old Pretender'), ought to assume the throne. But having been raised as a Catholic in France, James was entirely unacceptable to the Whig ruling elite. They therefore proposed to settle the line of succession on the Protestant heirs of Sophia, Electress of Hanover and granddaughter of James I. The Act of Settlement 1701 made provision for this, in one stroke putting paid to both divine right and hereditary monarchy.

By the time Prince Georg Ludwig, Sophia's son, assumed the throne in 1714 as George I, his powers had been significantly curtailed. Although the prerogatives of government remained vested in the crown, the king had to appoint Ministers who could manage Parliament and direct the administration. Elevating the Hanoverians accelerated this process. George I took little part in Cabinet meetings. No doubt his lack of English was something of a drawback but what he recognized more fundamentally was his lack of authority.

The constitutional impact was dramatic. Seventeenth-century conflicts between the crown and Parliament were replaced in the 18th century by tensions within Parliament itself. As competing factions vied for control of government, distinct political parties were formed. They therefore came into existence not as an expression of democracy but as vehicles for managing Parliament. As the emerging Whig and Tory parties became locked in ritualized conflict for control of government, the main practices of modern government—what Dicey later called 'constitutional conventions'—came into being.

The main functions of these constitutional conventions were twofold: first to transfer the exercise of the crown's prerogative powers to representative Ministers; and then to ensure that Ministers remained accountable to Parliament. The conventions of collective responsibility (the constitutional principle upholding Cabinet government) and individual ministerial responsibility (the constitutional principle requiring Ministers to account for all decisions of their departments) became central features of modern British constitutional arrangements. The traditional idea of a balance between monarchy, aristocracy, and commons was replaced by a balance between the parliamentary parties: between HM Government and HM Loyal Opposition.

Democratization

Nations are not primarily ruled by laws, still less by violence, as Burke noted in 1770. They are ruled by knowledge of the temper of a people and judicious management of it. The first duty of the statesman must therefore be to understand this temper, not least because the business of government must be exercised 'upon public principles and national grounds'. Burke therefore opposed any tendency of the crown to run government 'on the likings or prejudices, the intrigues or policies, of a court'. This is why he supported the emergence of political parties. A party, he explained, 'is a body of men united for promoting by their joint endeavours the national interest upon some particular principle in which they are all agreed'. Political parties ensure that politicians act in accordance with these principles rather than their own private considerations.

The form of government Burke was defending was aristocratic, confined to a small elite of landed families: he promoted the case for government of the people and for the people, but certainly not government by the people. Reinforcing this in a speech to the electors of Bristol in 1774, he explained that although a representative must listen to the wishes and opinions of his constituents, the idea that he would act on instruction or mandate was contrary to the whole tenor of the constitution. Parliament, he elaborated, was not a trading house of competing interests but a deliberative assembly of one nation, with one interest—the national interest. A representative could not sacrifice his judgement to the interests of his constituents; he must always be guided by the best interests of the nation. Parliament might be, in Coke's words, 'the grand inquest of the nation', but it was an inquest conducted only by our 'betters'.

The political struggles of the late 18th century were dominated by attempts to extend the franchise and reform the corrupt constituency system, a cause that was knocked back considerably by British reaction to the French Revolution. The sudden and violent extension of political rights to large sections of the French population led to the rise of anti-republican sentiment among the governing class and heightened awareness of the dangers of tampering with the intricate balances of 'the matchless constitution'. By the early 19th century, however, many felt that this wave of reaction was beginning to threaten the unity and stability of the British state. Writing in 1831, Hegel had argued that although the British constitution was to be admired for its achievements in reconciling authority and liberty, its constitutional development had become stultified. This was a direct consequence of its 18th-century achievements: the relative weakness of the monarchy together with the hegemony of the privileged landed class had removed the threat of absolutism, but it was also causing the aristocracy to ignore the interests of unpropertied workers.

This lack of national unity, which Hegel believed only the crown could provide, became a barrier to further evolution. The

18th-century elite might have accepted the principle of Blackstone's argument that the Act of Parliament 'can change and create afresh even the constitution of the kingdom', but it had seen no reason to do so with respect to the franchise. The breakthrough came only with the Reform Act of 1832.

Despite providing only a modest extension of the franchise, the 1832 Act marked the beginning of modern electoral reform. Extending the franchise to just over 5 per cent of the population, it could hardly be claimed as a great democratizing measure. It nonetheless marked a great constitutional turning point because, as a compromise measure that was devoid of principle, it paved the way for the gradual democratization of the Commons. The Representation of the People Act 1867, which doubled the size of the electorate, was more radical, but the 1832 Act had established the vital precedent that the franchise could be changed by statute. That the 1867 Act was introduced by a Tory government is significant: having accepted Bagehot's argument about England being a deferential country, the Tories had come round to the view that they could still win elections on an expanded franchise. Their convictions were later justified by the emergence of Tory working-class voters maintaining loyalty to the crown, which has since become a decisive electoral factor.

After 1867, the struggle to establish universal suffrage was marked by significant reforms in 1884, 1918, and the eventual realization of that goal in 1928. With the establishment of universal adult suffrage came the formation of disciplined political parties: Conservatives, Liberals, and, from the late 19th century, the Labour party. The growth of class consciousness, however, meant that these parties were perceived as representing sectional interests of society in the Commons. Such ideological divisions meant that the traditional idea of a balanced constitution between monarch, aristocracy, and the people was unsustainable. It was replaced by conflict, with the two hereditary elements of monarchy and aristocracy operating as a brake on the will of the elected chamber.

That conflict came to a head when the House of Lords—the hereditary chamber—rejected the Liberal government's budget in 1909. The so-called 'People's Budget' had proposed a super-tax on the wealthy and the introduction of death duties for the purpose of paying for the government's social reforms, including the introduction of old age pensions. The ensuing constitutional crisis was resolved only after two general elections in 1910: the first to assert the authority of the Commons over the Lords with respect to the budget and the second to assert the authority of the Commons over the king, who had refused to appoint 250 new Liberal peers to remove the inbuilt Conservative majority in the Lords without this again being tested at the polls. When the Liberals won both elections, the Lords reluctantly gave their consent to the Parliament Act 1911.

The 1911 Act removed the House of Lords' veto power. The necessity for their consent to 'money bills' was removed entirely and other Bills approved by the Commons in three successive sessions could receive the Royal Assent without the consent of the Lords, a procedure subsequently reduced to two successive sessions by the Parliament Act of 1949. The Commons was formally recognized as the pivot of modern constitutional government. Paradoxically, this moment of triumph also marked the beginning of the subversion of parliamentary authority. The Lords had rejected the 1909 budget, arguing that it needed to be submitted 'to the judgment of the country'. The 'people' thus made its first formal entry into constitutional discourse.

This principle of popular authority was subsequently generalized by Dicey. In 1914 he argued that 'a not unfairly elected legislature may misrepresent the permanent will of the electors' and might produce 'a machine which may well lead to political corruption'. With the coming of democratic majority government, Dicey, the most authoritative exponent of the legal doctrine of parliamentary sovereignty, started to unpick the logic of his own constitutional argument and to claim that the 'permanent will' of the people expressed a higher authority than that of Parliament.

Modern parliamentary practice

In *The English Constitution* (1867), Bagehot had identified five main functions of the House of Commons. The first and most important was to act as an electoral chamber: Parliament 'is the assembly which chooses our president [i.e. the Prime Minister]'. The second was expressive: to express 'the mind of the English people on all matters which come before it'. Third was the educative function, whereby this 'great and open council' must provide leadership and 'teach the nation what it does not know'. Fourthly, it had an informing function, of laying before the crown the grievances and complaints of sections of society. Finally there was the legislative function. Although neglecting the question of supply (i.e. approval of taxation), Bagehot's catalogue provides a useful template for assessing how the role of Parliament has altered since the Victorian era.

Over the last 150 years, the nature of government has been transformed. Modern government has greatly extended its range, assuming responsibility for improving social conditions by regulating economic activity and providing a wide range of public services. This great expansion poses a major challenge to the very idea of constitutionalism: devised as commitments to 'limited government', modern constitutions across the world have struggled to cope with the emergence of big government. The impact on Britain's evolutionary constitution may be gauged by changes in Parliament's role since Bagehot's day.

In specifying legislation as the last of his five functions, Bagehot was making a point. In the dignified version of the constitution, Parliament is the supreme, all-powerful legislature. But in the efficient—'what actually happens'—version, Parliament does not play any major role. Since the 19th century, Parliament has rarely made any major impact on the content of legislation. Responsibility for proposing and drafting the vast bulk of legislation rests with the government which, because of its parliamentary majority, is generally able to have its Bills enacted into law in the desired form. Parliament, it is sometimes argued, does not even engage in effective scrutiny of these Bills. This is partly because of the cumbersome nature both of debating procedures on the floor of the House and of arrangements for the detailed examination of Bills in standing committees. It is also because of their technical complexity, especially with the current tendency to provide a skeletal framework only in primary legislation, with details being delegated to the government to supply by way of executive legislation, such as Statutory Instruments. But it is also because of the sheer volume of legislation, much of it tabled in an unfinished form, which, given the pressures on the parliamentary timetable, provides little time for adequate consideration.

During the 20th century the number of Bills enacted in a parliamentary session has hardly changed. What has altered dramatically is the length and complexity of this legislation. In 1900, Parliament enacted 63 Acts amounting to fewer than 200 pages of the statute book. In 1950, only 51 Acts were passed but these took up over 1,000 pages. By 2000, the 45 Acts passed filled nearly 4,000 (larger-sized) pages of the statute book. And this is just the tip of the iceberg. The volume of executive legislation passed during the 20th century has grown tenfold: from around 300 Statutory Instruments (SIs) of under 1,000 pages in 1900 to 3,500 SIs amounting to over 10,000 pages in 2000. Since 1972, Parliament's powers with respect to legislation have been further circumscribed by its commitment to recognize European Union laws and to amend UK law to ensure compliance. Today, it is clear that only in a purely formal sense can Parliament be said to legislate. Legislation must be promoted through and approved by Parliament, but it may be more accurate to say that Parliament does not in any substantive sense legislate; it mainly legitimates.

The sheer volume of government-sponsored legislation has largely prevented Parliament from falling victim to American-style

2. The state opening of Parliament: the Queen's speech

'pork-barrel' politics in which votes are traded for constituency benefits. Such interest-trading does take place, but mainly through governmental consultation at the pre-legislative stage, a process which some political scientists characterize as post-parliamentary democracy. Over the last 150 years, then, legislative and policy action has shifted decisively from parliamentary to governmental processes.

This could not have occurred without a major expansion in governmental capacity. Hegel noted in 1831 that one of the factors undermining the unity of the British constitution was the absence of professional administrators trained to act in the public interest. It has been estimated, for example, that in 1815 the Home Secretary was ably assisted by just two under-secretaries and eighteen clerks. Since then we have seen a dramatic increase in administrative capacity. Basic reforms were introduced as a consequence of the Northcote–Trevelyan Report of 1854, which sought to eliminate the link between patronage and the exercise of administrative power by instituting a permanent non-political civil service recruited on merit through competitive examination. The creation of this professional civil service converted the binary separation of power—between government and Parliament—into a tripartite system in which the actions of both government and Parliament are disciplined and checked by the permanent administration of the country.

In the British system, Ministers are burdened with a vast catalogue of responsibilities ranging from initiating legislation and taking it through its parliamentary stages, policy-making, making executive decisions on all issues within their departmental remit, making appointments, handling complaints, managing their departments, and contributing to the formation of collective government policy. None of these tasks could be realized without the civil service. Civil servants ensure the seamless continuity of governmental business throughout changes in Ministries and also—given that their average term in office is only two years—in

Ministers. Behind every Minister is his or her alter ego, the official charged with the duty of offering advice and implementing decisions. This is the 'efficient secret' of the contemporary constitution. The British constitution works not merely because of the link between legislature and executive through the Cabinet system, but also because of the link between the transient (elected politicians) and the permanent (civil servants) in the running of the machinery of government.

This system works due to the emergence of the twin conventions of ministerial responsibility. The convention of collective responsibility rests on three main practices: *secrecy*, meaning that government decision-making should take place in private to encourage forthright discussion; *unanimity*, meaning that once a decision is made all members of the government must support it; and *confidence*, meaning that the government must retain the support of Parliament and must resign if it loses a vote of confidence. The convention of individual ministerial responsibility maintains that the Minister must answer publicly—and especially in Parliament—for all decisions of his or her department. The civil service facilitates the meshing of these two conventions. All government meetings must be held in the presence of officials who minute decisions and maintain records, thereby ensuring clarity, formality, and consistency. Governing with reference to precedents—itself an expression of the common law mentality—ensures the maintenance of probity and impartiality in the conduct of governmental business. It is bolstered by the convention of civil servant anonymity: to be able to serve all governments faithfully, civil servants should not be identified as playing a role in the shaping and making of governmental decisions.

Collective responsibility brings us back to the first of Bagehot's functions: Parliament's role in determining who will run the government. By convention, the queen must invite the person best able to form a government able to command the confidence of the Commons. A primary function of Parliament is to identify the

Prime Minister and to sustain that person in office, a task now delegated to the intricate workings of the party machines. This party machinery—the Whips' office and shadowy arrangements known as 'the usual channels'—not only controls the agenda of the Commons but also the fate of Ministers and Ministries. These 'efficient' party-controlled operations working through the 'dignified' conventions of responsibility have led many to the conclusion that there has been a 'waning of constitutional understanding': governmental decisions are now made through party mechanisms rather than in accordance with received constitutional understandings.

This point is exemplified in the role of the Prime Minister. The office is scarcely known to the law of the constitution; identified mainly through statutory powers given to the Prime Minister to make public appointments, the office itself is not defined by law. Yet, by combining leadership of the party with leadership of the government machine, it is on the verge of assuming a new type of monarchical status. The elevation of this office has come about partly through its powers of patronage, such as appointment and dismissal of Ministers. But it is also the result of the PM's contemporary role as both shaper and barometer of popular opinion. Monarchy is a type of strong government, Bagehot argued, primarily because it is intelligible government. 'The nature of a constitution, the action of an assembly, the play of parties, the unseen formation of a guiding opinion'—all of these, he claimed, are 'complex facts, difficult to know, and easy to mistake'. By contrast, 'the action of a single will, the fiat of a single mind, are easy ideas; anyone can make them out and no one can forget them'. In the modern world, the office of the monarch is subsumed within that of the Prime Minister.

In his introduction to a new edition of Bagehot in 1963, Richard Crossman gave expression to this shift. He contended that Cabinet government had been relegated to the dignified version of the constitution and replaced by a system of prime ministerial government. Crossman's thesis, which provoked considerable debate, reached its apotheosis in the Thatcher (1979–91) and Blair (1997–2007) administrations. In the Blair government, Cabinets met less frequently, for shorter periods, and with fewer papers to consider than under any period since 1900. Instead, government policy was regularly made by the Prime Minister in informal, bilateral, and unminuted meetings with Ministers, briefed by his own special advisers rather than career civil servants. This mode of 'sofa government', more resonant of a monarchical court than a presidential style of government, renders parliamentary accountability difficult, a point highlighted by the exposure of serious weaknesses in decision-making with respect to the Iraq war of 2003. In this type of regime, the power of the PM is barely limited if his or her standing in the opinion polls is high. But when those ratings plummet then, as the experiences of Thatcher, Blair, and Brown illustrate, power dissipates and they are forced to rely on the support of power-holders within the party.

If Parliament's influence in choosing the Prime Minister and making laws has waned, so too has its authority in other ways. A series of scandals—ranging from 'cash for questions' in the 1990s, 'cash for honours' in 2006–7, and MPs' parliamentary expenses in 2009—has greatly diminished the standing of Parliament in the eyes of the public. Once a jealous protector of its own unique privileges—underpinned by the provision in the Bill of Rights that no proceedings in Parliament can be questioned in any court—members' expenses are now policed by an Independent Parliamentary Standards Authority established by the Parliamentary Standards Act of 2009.

Are these developments leading to the destruction of the traditional constitution that Bagehot in his fear of democracy foretold? Has the 'rule of money… working upon ignorance for its own ends' now managed to 'spoil our Parliament' and undermine the constitution? Before yielding to such pessimism, we might take note of one important parliamentary function that Bagehot underplayed: Parliament's role in testing Ministers through debates, questions, and other forms of scrutiny. This remains Parliament's saving feature. Behind the ritualized arrangements of Government and Opposition, through which much of the business of Parliament is conducted, Parliament continues to perform an important role in demanding openness in government, promoting high standards of ministerial probity and competence, and maintaining a nursery of ambitious MPs who, through constant testing, acquire the experience needed to become effective Ministers.

Chapter 4

The expansion and contraction of the English state

> We cannot get on without the State, or the Nation, or the
> Commonwealth, or the Public, and yet that is what we are
> proposing to do.
>
> F. W. Maitland, 1901.

> What should they know of England who only England know?
>
> Rudyard Kipling, 1891.

Modern constitutional democracies commonly possess a
constitution drafted in the name of 'the people' who establish a
system of government relating to a clearly defined territory. But
with respect to the British case, the territory, the people, and the
governing principles they are supposed to have authorized are all
matters of considerable ambiguity. The reason lies in the nature of
the state which has its seat of government in London. This
state—the United Kingdom of Great Britain and Northern
Ireland—has a complex history.

England, Britain, United Kingdom

As the largest, most powerful nation on the islands, the English
have always sought to dominate the Irish, Scots, and Welsh,
primarily to maintain the security of their state. After 1066, Wales
was rapidly absorbed into the English state. This was achieved by

a brutal policy of conquest brought to a formal conclusion by the Statute of Wales of 1535 by which Welsh lands were absorbed into the English shire system and the English common law applied throughout England and Wales. The story with respect to the Scots and Irish is more complicated. Throughout modern political history, the Scots and Irish have used—and been used by—other European powers as part of an ongoing island struggle, often tangled up in questions of religious allegiance.

Scotland. The essential point about Anglo-Scottish relations is that the union between the two nations was forged not by conquest but by treaty. In 1707, Scotland and England were joined by the Treaty of Union to create the United Kingdom of Great Britain. But this was the culmination of a longer process. Consider, for example, the issue of ethnicity. Lowland Scots once saw themselves as part of a common Saxon heritage. For them the critical division within Britain was not that between English and Scot, or Saxon and Celt, but between Saxon and Norman. Lowland Scots shared with their English counterparts the narrative of maintaining Saxon liberty against the threat of the Norman Yoke. Having little in common with the feudal organization of Highland clans, they shared the Saxon distaste for Norman attempts to impose feudalism. From the 16th century onwards, this ethnically orientated unionist narrative was overlaid with a religious aspect as the Reformation placed Scotland and England in the community of Protestant nations. Consequently, when in 1603 James VI of Scotland acceded to the English throne as James I, the seeds of union had already been sown.

The union of the crowns provided the catalyst for further debate about the benefits of union, but the main innovation was that of bringing the political and commercial aspects of the question into consideration along with the religious. During the revolutionary upheavals of the mid-17th century, for example, the Scots even proposed ecclesiastical union of the British people along Presbyterian lines. And the 1689 revolutionary settlement could be seen not merely as the restoration of the ancient constitution but also the institutionalization of Scots Presbyterian principles.

But the eventual union in 1707 came about in inauspicious circumstances. Having in 1701 turned to the Hanoverian line to resolve the royal succession crisis, the English were concerned that the Scots would not follow suit and might restore the Jacobite line, thereby opening up the possibility of intense conflict. Union was one means of avoiding this. At the same time, the Scots were vulnerable: following the utter failure of their own imperial enterprise (Darien, or New Caledonia, in the Caribbean), they desperately needed access to trade and empire and this was the carrot the English dangled before them. The outcome, expressed in the 1707 settlement, was the establishment of a common set of legislative, executive, and fiscal—though not judicial—arrangements for the new kingdom of Great Britain.

Some Scots jurists have argued that the Treaty of Union is fundamental law and takes the form of a modern constitutional settlement. These arguments have only been made in the last fifty or so years, before which no one seemed to question the fact that this was an incorporating union founded on parliamentary sovereignty. Following the Treaty, 45 Scottish MPs and 16 representative peers simply joined the Westminster Parliament without even a general election being held, making the point unequivocally that Scotland had been incorporated into an Anglo-centric British state. As Dicey expressed it, 'neither the Act of Union with Scotland, nor the Dentists Act, 1878, has more claim than the other to be considered a supreme law'. Guarantees were certainly provided in the Articles of Union to protect the distinctive legal and educational systems and the Presbyterian system of church government. But these were statements of political intent without binding status, and some—such as the requirement that Scottish university professors be practising members of the Church of Scotland—have been overridden by ordinary legislation without contention.

Ireland. Union with Ireland was altogether different. Ireland had from the 12th century onwards been subject to Norman and then English attempts at domination. At first, this was achieved through military campaigns, but these assumed a new level of intensity after the English Reformation when the English took more direct governmental control. This was achieved through colonization, that is through a governmental policy of land confiscation and plantation, by which Irish lands were handed over to English and Scottish Protestant settlers. By the end of the 17th century, the land possessions of Anglo-Protestant settler landlords amounted to 85 per cent of the country. They also acquired complete control of the Irish Parliament, passing a series of penal laws that imposed severe political and civil disabilities on the vast majority of Irish Catholics who refused to convert to Protestantism. By 1690, with the defeat of James II's army—supported by Irish Catholics—at the Battle of the Boyne, the Protestant Ascendancy was complete.

Throughout the period of conquest and colonization, the Irish Parliament had been preserved, though it remained a dependent legislature. This dependency was formally expressed in Poynings's Law of 1494, which determined that the Irish Parliament could meet only when authorized by the (English) king and which required all legislation to receive prior approval of the English Privy Council. Poynings's Law ensured that only legislation compatible with English law and acceptable to English interests was admitted to the Irish statute book. Dependency was further entrenched by the Dependency of Ireland Act of 1720, which declared that the British Parliament maintained 'full power and authority to make laws and statutes of sufficient validity to bind the Kingdom and people of Ireland'. This measure confirmed Ireland's colonial status and also frustrated the aspirations of Irish Protestants to acquire constitutional equality with the English. After the 1798 Rebellion of United Irishmen, which had been influenced by the republican ideals of the American and French revolutions, the British determined that the only lasting foundation for security lay in the union of Ireland with Britain. In 1801 the Irish Parliament was dissolved and incorporated into the Westminster Parliament. In a formal sense, a new state—the United Kingdom of Great Britain and Ireland—was created. The 1801 Act, marking the apotheosis of the principle of parliamentary sovereignty, unified legal authority throughout the British Isles.

This new state was cursed from the outset. Prime Minister Pitt had quietly conceded Catholic emancipation as part of the Union negotiations. After the Irish Parliament had been dissolved, however, George III vetoed this proposal, claiming that it contravened his coronation oath to preserve the Protestant religion. The king's action made Pitt's position impossible and he immediately resigned. But the king's manoeuvre had ensured that in the eyes of the great majority of the Irish population the Union entirely lacked legitimacy. Right from the outset, the Irish lobbied first for Catholic emancipation (achieved in 1829), and then for home rule.

Irish Home Rule, the attempt to reconcile the aspirations of Irish nationalism within the frame of the British state, became the dominant political issue of the late 19th century. Home Rule Bills were rejected in 1886 and 1893, causing a fundamental split within the Liberal Party. When a third Bill was eventually introduced in 1912, it was enacted in the face of Lords' opposition only through the procedures of the Parliament Act 1911. The resulting delay led to its suspension because of the war, which gave time for the Ulster Protestants vehemently opposed to home rule to raise a private army. The formation of this army, financed by leading Conservatives and Unionists, was justified on the grounds that the Liberal Government had 'seized upon despotic power by fraud' (Bonar Law) and that such a despotic use of power 'might justify what was technically conspiracy or rebellion' (Dicey).

As it turned out, the threat of sedition in Ulster was overtaken by events. The failure of the Irish Party, despite its huge majority

3. John Redmond, leader of the Irish party, and Home Rule, 1911

support in Ireland, to achieve through parliamentary means what it had been seeking since 1885 contributed to frustrations and splits. What followed in quick succession was the Easter Rising in 1916, the electoral success of Sinn Féin, the formation of the Dáil, the Irish War of Independence (1919–21), and then the Anglo-Irish Treaty by which Ireland—with the exception of the six counties of Northern Ireland—seceded from the UK. Consequently, the only part of the Government of Ireland Act 1920 to be implemented was—ironically—home rule within the British state for the six counties of Northern Ireland which maintained a Protestant and Unionist majority.

Empire

Constitutional historians often treat the 18th century as a period of quiescence. After extended 17th-century conflict, the British experienced stability; there may have been abortive Jacobite insurrections in 1715 and 1745, but there were no great revolutions. In this period of relative stability, the basic conventions of modern parliamentary government were forged. But this is a purely domestic view: a rather different picture emerges from a geo-political perspective. Between 1688 and 1815 a dramatic change occurred in the nature of the British state. Britain was not only transformed from an agrarian to an industrial society but from a relatively weak, insular state into a major European power. During this era, Britain established a standing army and navy, engaged in what has been called the Second Hundred Years War against France, and acquired an extensive empire. The creation of Great Britain in 1707 led in the following century to the formation of what imperialists called 'Greater Britain'.

The basic thesis of Sir John Seeley's influential lectures on *The Expansion of England* (1883) was that the British Empire was fundamentally different from the ancient empires of the Persians, Romans, or Turks. Founded mainly on settlement rather than conquest, 'Greater Britain is a real enlargement of the English State' and it 'carries across the seas not merely the

English race but the authority of the English Government'. Wherever the English people are, there is England: in New England, New Jersey, and New York (and British people, too, in New South Wales and Nova Scotia). Unlike other major empires, there was no (Rationalist) imperial project: 'We seem, as it were, to have conquered and peopled half the world in a fit of absence of mind.'

Seeley's point was that in its original incarnation the British Empire was founded on colonial settlement. Its hub was in North America, where the settlers' intention had been to transplant a liberal version of English governmental arrangements. Unlike in Ireland, these colonies did not have native Parliaments, but the dictates of geography meant that in practice they possessed great autonomy. Tensions in imperial relations emerged, however, once the Revolution of 1688 established the principle of the sovereign authority of the Westminster Parliament. Formally global and absolute, Parliament did not always recognize that this principle must be tempered by practical—perhaps even constitutional—considerations.

The critical issue concerned financing of the military. Having modernized military finance at home by replacing feudal tenure (with its attendant military service) with parliamentary grants raised through taxation, the question arose whether a contribution to these costs should be imposed on the colonies. But in levying taxation that was not subject to approval by colonial assemblies, Parliament seemed to be depriving the colonists of the same safeguards it had struggled over centuries to maintain at home. When the Westminster Parliament refused to yield, 13 of the 18 American colonies raised armies and in 1776 declared themselves independent. After eight years of war, Britain was obliged to recognize their independence.

The success of the American Revolution irrevocably altered the constitutional arrangements of the British settler empire. The authority of the crown remained the formal principle but it was now tempered by the clear practical limitations of London's capacity to govern from the metropolis. During the 19th century, the overriding issue for settler colonies was restrictions on their powers of self-government, illustrated by the extensive powers given to appointed governors. But from mid-century, following the Durham Report of 1839, powers of responsible government were gradually conferred on the settler colonies, leading to the creation of the Dominions of Canada in 1867, Australia in 1901, New Zealand in 1907, and South Africa in 1910. This constituted an unparalleled devolution of power by an imperial authority. Later, by virtue of the Statute of Westminster of 1931, the Westminster Parliament declared that it would no longer legislate for a Dominion without its request and consent, thereby relinquishing its untrammelled authority across the Empire. Settler colonies had, to all intents and purposes, become autonomous states within the British Commonwealth of Nations.

Alongside settler colonies, a 'second British empire' grew up: this was an empire of conquest rather than settlement. This is not to overlook the point that the foundation of settler colonies had resulted in the displacement—even genocide—of aboriginal populations, or indeed the extent to which these liberal arrangements of settler self-government were underpinned by the institution of slavery. The point is merely that this second empire was explicitly founded on authoritarian rule over subordinate peoples. Driven by commerce, trade, and resource exploitation, this empire spanned the Caribbean, Africa, Asia, and beyond, an empire on which the sun never set. From the constitutional perspective, India provides the exemplary case.

The East India Company had acquired responsibility for English commercial interests in India for over 150 years before 1757, when it began to make territorial acquisitions, bringing parts of India under its governing control. From that moment, the Company was subject to regulation by legislation, but only in 1848 was it wound up and India brought into the Empire. The conquest of India was therefore not formally an act of state and India never became a tributary state: taxation drawn from India was spent on the government of India. But the rights and obligations attendant on imperial conquest generated considerable debate, which took place under the banner of 'liberalism and empire'. How could this 'second empire' founded on military conquest, racial subjection, and territorial acquisition be justified in the light of British constitutional values of liberty, equality, and the rule of law?

One answer was that representative institutions could work only in societies that had reached a certain level of civilization, until which point authoritarian government was required. Imperial government was therefore justified on the ground that expert rule by British officials unchecked by colonial assemblies provided the surest means of bringing material improvement and progress, the preconditions of liberty and equality. Leading utilitarians, such as James Mill, his son J. S. Mill, and Macaulay, all worked for the East India Company and were kept busy promoting law reform in India. Unable to achieve reform at home owing to the power and vested interest of the landed class, they promoted formal legislative codes to modernize India's penal, land, and revenue laws.

But whatever the utilitarian justification for imperialism, might not authoritarian rule abroad corrupt liberal practices at home? This concern was most clearly expressed by Burke, who argued that the growth of British power in India also threatened British liberties. The financial corruption, brutality of rule, and massive wealth generated by officials of the East India Company not only institutionalized authoritarianism abroad but also undermined British constitutional values at home. Having exploited the natives in India, these wealthy traders returned to Britain and insinuated their mercenary logic into the fabric of British political life by buying seats in Parliament and upsetting the balance of the constitution. For Burke, imperial instincts were antithetical to British constitutional values.

Burke's arguments had little impact on British imperial ambition, but they did influence the manner of governing. Where liberal imperialists saw a barbaric society needing the blessings of civilization, Burke recognized a morality and culture different from—but equal to—that of the west. There was an unresolved tension in the practices of imperial government. Should the British seek modernization through formal legal instruments or work within the grain of local culture and practice? British rule remained fixed on maintaining 'peace, order and good government'. But should this be achieved by the imposition of modern forms of law or should native laws be retained and respected? British practice always tended to accommodate indigenous ways and collaborate with indigenous elites: how else could a handful of colonial officials govern? Drawing on the African experience in particular, this practice later became known as 'indirect rule'. But it had been the guiding principle throughout: maximize experience and minimize rationalistic, modernizing governmental schemes.

A similar pragmatism shaped the ways in which territories evolved from crown colonies to self-government. During the First World War—a war which the British Empire entered as a single entity—India mutated into a modified Dominion, leading to dyarchy in the inter-war period (in which elected Indian Ministers assumed responsibility for a range of domestic tasks) and eventually to independence in 1949. That India—and others—were able to form republics yet remain in the Commonwealth owes much to what had been learned from the complications of Anglo-Irish post-1914 history. The Second World War marked a watershed. The self-governing nations of the Empire had entered the war through declarations of their own Parliaments, itself indicative of the loosening of imperial bonds. Immediately after the war the process of self-government and independence for the vast majority of Britain's fifty-two dependent territories commenced. Britain maintained supervisory responsibility for long enough to be involved in the drafting of independence constitutions. This was a delicate exercise, especially with respect to protections for minorities—ethnic, religious, linguistic—in the new state, and the difficulties entailed in the export of the Westminster system of government were greatly underestimated. Although the new constitutions were invariably drafted on the parliamentary model, many were subsequently amended and presidential systems established.

How does this potted history of empire help illuminate the workings of the British constitution? The most important point is this: throughout a period of dramatic growth in both the scale and complexity of the British Empire, its legal form remained permanently fixed. Sovereignty was illimitable and perpetual. This meant that, since no limits on the authority of the Crown-in-Parliament were conceivable, changing relations between the metropolis and the peripheries had to be effected informally and pragmatically, by political and administrative rather than legal methods. The word that remained taboo was that of federalism, entailing a written constitution, the formal demarcation of jurisdictional responsibility between the centre and the peripheries, and the establishment of a supreme court to police the division. Federalism in all its forms was anathema to British constitutional thought, whether with respect to relations between the several nations of the British Isles or between the imperial authority and its dependent colonies.

European Union

The challenge of federalism, albeit in another guise, has come to dominate post-war constitutional discussion. The UK was not a founder signatory to the Treaty of Rome (1957) which created the European Economic Community (EEC), later the European Community (EC) and most recently the European Union (EU). Because of its imperial legacy and close trading ties to British Commonwealth countries, the UK did not then consider its primary economic relations to lie within Europe. Overlying this was the feeling that membership would entail a loss of national sovereignty, something that—being bound up in centuries of constitutional rhetoric—could not be contemplated.

During the 1960s, however, views about trading relations changed and the UK, led by a Conservative government, eventually joined the EEC in 1973. Concerns about the implications of membership caused the incoming Labour government in 1975 to undertake a novel constitutional experiment. A referendum was held on whether the UK should remain in the Community, with 67.2 per cent. answering in the affirmative. But controversy over the loss of national sovereignty— what Hugh Gaitskell in 1962 had called 'the end of a thousand years of history'—has permeated debate ever since.

The European Communities Act 1972, giving effect in domestic law to the 'new legal order' of Community law, was a masterpiece of concise legislative drafting and few grasped its radical implications. It stated that all rights and obligations 'from time to time arising by or under the Treaties...are without further enactment to be given legal effect'. Since such rights and obligations included those declared by rulings of the European Court of Justice (ECJ), they included two basic principles not found in the Treaty itself but whose significance cannot be overstated.

The first is the principle of the *supremacy of European law*. The transfer of rights and duties to the Community, the Court declared in 1964, 'carries with it a permanent limitation of their sovereign rights, against which a subsequent unilateral act incompatible with the concept of the Community cannot prevail'. In other words, in the event of a conflict between the law of a member state and any provision of European law, the latter must prevail. The second principle is that of *direct effect*. European law not only creates obligations on states that are enforceable in international law, it also confers rights and obligations that can be directly enforced by individuals in the courts of member states. This means that individual citizens can bring actions in domestic courts arguing that a domestic law should not be applied because it conflicts with European law. Given the scope and potential impact of these principles, it was difficult to avoid the conclusion that the untrammelled authority of the Crown-in-Parliament to make law had been seriously compromised.

Despite the ECJ's claim of 'permanent limitation', it is clear that any future Parliament can repeal the 1972 Act and withdraw from the European Union: in that sense ultimate national sovereignty is retained. But short of this 'nuclear option', the UK is now locked into a 'federal' arrangement that requires the sharing of law-making authority. With the growth in EU membership, decision-making processes have had to be streamlined. Majority voting is now standard, meaning that new rules and regulations no longer require the agreement of all member states; subject to certain exceptions, no member state possesses the power of veto. And with this evolution, the claim that Parliament retains final law-making authority over any aspect of social or economic regulation is tenuous.

In addition to these political concerns about control over law-making processes, there is a technical point about the legal doctrine of sovereignty. Despite the ECJ's supremacy principle, British constitutional practice requires that, in the event of a conflict between statutory provisions, the most recently enacted legislation prevails. So if, say, the Merchant Shipping Act of 1988 conflicts with the provisions of the Treaty of Rome, which is given legal effect in domestic law by virtue of the European Communities Act of 1972, which law applies? Community law requires the Treaty to prevail, but constitutional practice suggests the 1988 Act takes priority. After years of avoiding this controversy, the English courts finally resolved it in the early 1990s. In the *Factortame* litigation, the House of Lords suspended the operation of the Merchant Shipping Act after the ECJ had ruled that its provisions were contrary to obligations in the Treaty of Rome. 'Whatever limitation of its sovereignty Parliament accepted when it enacted the European Communities Act 1972', the court held, 'was entirely voluntary.'

This ruling generated fierce debate among constitutional lawyers. Leading the traditionalists was Sir William Wade, who claimed that the 'Parliament of 1972 had succeeded in binding the Parliament of 1988 and restricting its sovereignty, something that was supposed to be constitutionally impossible'. But the modernizers contended that the ruling merely illustrated their more general claim that constitutional law cannot be reduced to the simple rule that whatever Parliament enacts is law. Constitutional law, they argued, is a more complex concept, more like a structure of 'sovereign' constitutional principles. Respect for Parliament's enactments is certainly an important principle. But the delegation of law-making authority to the EU does not in itself amount to a sharing of sovereignty, not least because this delegation is itself authorized by the sovereign Parliament.

This technical dispute became the catalyst for a general debate about the law of the constitution, a debate to which we will return in the following chapters. In the UK, the doctrine of parliamentary sovereignty has acquired an almost sacred status, bolstering the informal, pragmatic, administrative character of British governmental practice. The EU is a governmental entity entirely foreign to the English temperament. The EU is what Germans call a *Rechtsgemeinschaft*, a community of law. Lacking all those elements—shared history and culture, and common language—that infuse the traditional idea of constitutional ordering, the EU binds member states solely through the medium of formal law. Lacking the military or fiscal resources of nation-states, its primary medium of domination is that of legal rule-making. The EU has propagated a new species: 'Eurolegalism', marked by strictly defined, purposive rules to regulate governmental action and relying heavily on formal, judicial oversight and enforcement mechanisms. As a legal construct, the EU is in fact an expression of hyper-Rationalism that runs directly counter to the traditions of British constitutional practice.

Devolution

The Labour government elected in 1997 came to power with an agenda for 'constitutional modernization'. Central to that programme was the devolution of power to the non-English parts of the United Kingdom. With respect to Scotland and Wales, this policy was a legacy of eighteen years of Conservative rule in which radical changes like de-industrialization, privatization, de-regulation, and restructuring of the welfare state had failed to find support in the Celtic regions, leaving the government with scarcely enough of those MPs to run the Scottish and Welsh Offices. The legitimacy deficit was most strongly felt in Scotland where a Claim of Right was drafted in 1989, asserting the 'sovereign right of the Scottish people to determine the form of Government best suited to their needs'. Endorsed by 58 of Scotland's 72 MPs, 7 of their 8 Members of the European Parliament, 59 of the 65 local councils, and numerous churches, trade unions, and civil bodies, the Claim led to the establishment of an (unofficial) Scottish Constitutional Convention which drew up a scheme for home rule. This provided the template for the Labour government's proposals.

The government's devolution programme was implemented in the Scotland Act 1998, a scheme of devolved legislative powers to a Scottish Parliament in Edinburgh, and the Government of Wales Act 1998, a scheme of devolved executive powers to a National Assembly for Wales in Cardiff (though subsequently extended in accordance with further legislation in 2006). The 1998 Acts had been preceded by referendums in Scotland and Wales. Although the Scottish referendum yielded a resoundingly positive result (75:25), the Welsh voted in favour of an Assembly by the narrowest of margins (50.3:49.7).

During the same year, the Northern Ireland Act was passed. This established a Northern Ireland Assembly with devolved legislative powers. But the situation here, as ever, was fundamentally different. After the post-First World War upheavals in Ireland, in 1922 a Parliament with devolved powers of home rule had been established for Northern Ireland. In common with decolonization arrangements, this Parliament at Stormont replicated Westminster practices. In the tense conditions in which a sizeable minority rejected the legitimacy of the arrangement, however, the Protestant majority ran the province to the benefit of their own community. When the grievances of the Catholic minority were turned into civil rights campaigns of the late 1960s, tension was strained to breaking point. After violence erupted, the British government and army became increasingly involved in the domestic affairs of the province, and in 1972 the Stormont Parliament was suspended and later abolished. The 1998 Act thus marked the end of a period of direct rule from London. And the settlement it introduced was much more than a scheme of legislative devolution: deploying Rationalist principles of institutional design, it signalled nothing less than a systematic attempt to promote social change through a constitution-building exercise.

The backdrop to these reforms was the Belfast (or Good Friday) Agreement signed by the UK and Irish governments in 1998, marking the outcome of a peace process. Ratified by referendums in both Ireland and the North, it initiated a constitutional process designed to encourage nationalists and unionists to work together to govern the province. The establishment of an Executive containing both sides of 'the community' and governing as a dyarchy forms one of three strands of the Agreement; the others provide for a North–South Ministerial Council for discussion and implementation of limited shared executive functions, and a British–Irish Intergovernmental Conference to develop longer-term strategy.

Each side has accepted that the majority of the people of Northern Ireland wish to remain part of the UK and that they have the right to self-determination, including the right to secede should this be the wish of a future majority. But the Agreement also aims to bolster the legitimacy of constitutional arrangements within the province through initiatives that include the decommissioning of paramilitary weapons, prisoner release schemes, the reconstitution of the police and prosecution services, the regulation of symbols and parades, and the strengthening of equality laws. The adoption of traditional Westminster practices since the 1920s is now widely recognized as having exacerbated the political problems in the province and novel constitutional techniques now form the central plank of a solution.

These various schemes for devolution in Scotland, Wales, and Northern Ireland have created a mosaic, with the governing arrangements for each of the non-English parts of the UK now varying widely. In one sense, this is typical, being resonant of the old imperial practice of 'indirect rule'. What is more puzzling is the claim that these developments reflect a process of 'constitutional modernization'. Each scheme undoubtedly contains modernizing elements, evident in voting systems, rules of assembly procedure, or executive decision-making arrangements. In that sense these reforms mark the renewal of regional politics. But reforms that strengthen legitimacy in the regions must raise questions of legitimacy at the centre. The Westminster Parliament no longer legislates for the domestic affairs of the whole of the UK. A UK government can no longer pledge, for example, to reform the National Health Service when, outside England, it lacks leverage to do so. How do we make sense of the role of the 'mother of parliaments', when non-English MPs can vote on—and vote down—legislation to reform the health service in England yet English MPs have relinquished their authority in such matters with respect to the rest of Britain?

One answer to this conundrum is that devolution legislation explicitly states that the establishment of subordinate legislatures does not affect the continuing sovereign authority of the UK Parliament. Technically, the Westminster Parliament can still legislate on matters within the competence of the Scottish

Parliament or Northern Ireland Assembly. Formally, the doctrine of parliamentary sovereignty remains unaffected. But in practice the situation is more complicated. In relation to Scotland, for example, the UK Parliament has accepted the convention that it will legislate on devolved matters only with the consent of the Scottish Parliament. Given the authority of the Scottish Parliament, it is difficult to envisage the circumstances in which the UK Parliament could do so without that consent. Nor in reality can the UK Parliament repeal the Scotland Act without the consent of the Scottish Parliament. If it sought to do so, the Scots would assert that they have their own Parliament and governing arrangements and should reclaim their independence. We may not yet have a federal arrangement for Britain, but the omnipotence of the Westminster Parliament delineated by constitutional lawyers since the 18th century exists no longer.

State, nation, and citizen

State, nation, and citizen are three essentially modern concepts and none of them easily fits the British experience. In the modern narrative, the people of a defined territory conceive themselves to form a unity (a nation) and they establish an association (a state) of which they become equal members (citizens). The essential terms of this association are then expressed in a basic pact, the written constitution that takes effect as fundamental law. In reality, states are invariably constructed from above. But in this singular moment of imaginative constitutional self-reflection, the people conceive themselves to be authors of their own governing arrangements. We can surely maintain a certain scepticism towards any such idealized representation but still recognize that moment as the founding act of modern constitutionalism.

Yet each of these three elements confounds our understanding of the British experience. The British have never really embraced the idea of the state as an expression of the institutional form of the association. The closest legal symbol is the crown, which signifies the monarch in her public capacity. It is in this sense that we refer to Her Majesty's government, or to crown servants, or the Royal Courts of Justice. But the jurisprudence surrounding the concept of the crown remains blurred, and no easy distinction can be made between monarch and crown, person and office, private and public.

This obfuscation permeates the laws of nationality and citizenship. English law is tied to ancient bonds of allegiance, by which subjects owed fealty to their king. This has its roots in *Calvin's Case* (1608), in which it was held that those born in Scotland after the accession of James VI (of Scotland) to the throne of England (as James I) were naturalized in England and entitled to the full protection of its law. Recognition of allegiance as a personal bond meant that all the peoples of the Empire became subjects of the king. This absence of a modern law of citizenship presented particular difficulties as a consequence of various waves of Commonwealth immigration from the mid-20th century onwards, and this led to the modern law of British citizenship being shaped mainly by the exigencies of immigration control.

The present position with respect to citizenship is very complicated. The Immigration Act 1971 divided the main citizenship status categories—Citizen of the United Kingdom and Colonies, British subject without citizenship of any Commonwealth country, and British Protected Person—between patrials and non-patrials, with only the former category (those with a close birth tie to Britain) having the right of abode. That law was reformed in the British Nationality Act 1981, which established five new categories—British Citizen, British Dependent Territories Citizen, British Overseas Citizen, British Subject, and British Protected Person—with only the first category carrying with it a right of abode. This is complicated enough, but it becomes even more intricate because the attendant rights of citizenship are not linked to these status categories in a systematic manner: rights to vote, to stand for office, and to work in the public service are, for example, given not only to most categories of British citizens and subjects but also to citizens of the Republic of Ireland and the British Commonwealth. Yet for the purposes of the EU, the definition of British nationality refers only to a British Citizen and almost all other categories of British passport-holders or Commonwealth citizens are excluded.

The general point is that the law of the constitution remains fixed within a monarchical conception of authority and it has not been systematically adapted to modern notions of the state, nation, or citizen. In this chapter, I have recounted how the English state (which covered England and Wales) during the 18th century was transformed into a British state founded on Protestantism and set to work to build an empire. As one of its first colonial projects, Ireland has never been fully integrated, and in that sense there has never really been a UK state. This is evidenced today by the peculiar status of Northern Ireland, which the British state is pledged to relinquish once a majority of the population of the province signals that preference. In the light of evident pressures for 'modernization', the big question that remains is whether, now that Britain's imperial mission is over and a religious basis of political identity seems anachronistic, the British state any longer has a rationale.

Modern constitutions establish unitary or federal systems of government. France is a unitary model, in which there is a logical arrangement of local administration united around an authoritative centre. The United States, in which the limits to the authority of states and the federal government are set by the Constitution, exemplifies the federal model. But the British state is neither unitary nor federal. The Scots might prefer to call it an asymmetrically federal arrangement; others call it a union state—rather than a unitary state—on the grounds that different governing arrangements exist with respect to the several territories within the state. Such labelling suggests we are still searching for a logic at work and, as Maitland once said, the English are not elementary enough to be logical.

It might even be the case that the British way of muddling through is best suited to the challenges ahead. This, though, will never satisfy constitutional modernizers. If Britain is a democracy in which power is exercised in the name of the people, can the crown still offer an adequate symbol of state? Although we have long lived with the political notion of a British people, to what extent is this the product of a shared imperial venture which, given the loss of empire, no longer makes sense? This is precisely the question which is now to be tested in a referendum on independence for Scotland scheduled for autumn 2014. And which way do the people of Northern Ireland face: south to the Irish Republic or east to Scotland? That too could be the subject of some future referendum. The Treaty of Lisbon of 2009, it might be noted, requires the EU to respect the 'constitutional identity' of its member states. But do the British still possess the confidence to specify that identity?

Chapter 5
Civil liberty

It is the land that freemen till,
That sober-suited Freedom chose,
The land, where girt with friends or foes
Man may speak the thing he will;

A land of settled government,
A land of just and old renown,
Where Freedom broadens slowly down
From precedent to precedent

Alfred Lord Tennyson, 1842.

Throughout the modern era the British constitution has attracted high praise for the value it places on liberty. This theme featured most prominently in the work of Whig constitutional historians for whom liberties were never simply the product of monarchical concession but were, in Blackstone's words, 'coeval with our form of government'. Liberties might occasionally have been suppressed by overbearing kings, but 'the vigour of our free constitution has always delivered the nation from these embarrassments' and has always managed to resettle 'the balance of our rights and liberties...to its proper level'. The great landmark documents—Magna Carta (1215), the Petition of Right (1628), the Bill of Rights (1689)—conferred no new rights. They merely restated their existence as, in the words of the Bill of Rights, 'the true, ancient and indubitable rights of the people of this kingdom'. It is this tradition of conduct that led Montesquieu to claim in 1748 that Britain was the 'one nation in the world whose constitution had political liberty for its direct purpose'.

This chapter has three main objectives. It first examines the nature of these liberties and the arrangements by which they are protected. In this respect, it sketches the manner in which (understood cumulatively) 'civil liberty' has been maintained. Secondly, it considers the extent to which the modern extension in the powers of government has eroded these traditional safeguards. Finally, it assesses the significance of recent judicial and legislative developments that, in response to the growing powers of government, aim to restore the protection of liberty. The question the reader might bear in mind throughout is whether Montesquieu's claim can still be made: does the contemporary constitution have 'political liberty for its direct purpose'?

The constitution of liberty

The basic liberties protected by the constitution were defined by Blackstone in three main categories. First, there is the right of *personal security*, which protects the life, bodily integrity, health, and reputation of the person. From this basic right evolve the rules of criminal law, poor law provision for the necessities of life, and the law of defamation. Second is the right to *personal liberty*, guaranteeing freedom from imprisonment without due cause and lawful trial, and freedom of movement within and without the realm. The final category is the right of *private property*, which includes the free use, enjoyment, and disposition of property regulated only by the law of the land, including taxation by parliamentary authorization.

Recognizing the need for the constitution to secure their effective protection, Blackstone noted that these rights are safeguarded by certain institutional 'pillars of liberty'. The most important of these is

Parliament. Parliament imposes limitations on the king's prerogatives, seeks the redress of grievances before acquiescing in taxation, and maintains the Englishman's right of access to the courts for remedying wrongs. But other institutional arrangements are of critical importance, and two in particular. The first is trial by jury, i.e. judgement by one's peers. This provision, rooted in ancient Saxon practice, is claimed to stem from ch. 39 of Magna Carta: 'No freeman shall be taken or imprisoned...except by the legal judgment of his peers or by the law of the land.' The second arrangement, which also stems from ch. 39, is the writ of habeas corpus, by which the court requires that legal cause for detention be shown. During the Victorian era, these auxiliary protections—overseen by a judiciary whose independence had been signalled by s. 3 of the Act of Settlement of 1701—were transformed by Dicey into a formal constitutional principle. He called this principle the 'rule of law'.

For Dicey, the rule of law has three meanings. First, no one can be punished except for a 'distinct breach of the law established in the ordinary legal manner before the ordinary Courts of the land'. Dicey here highlights the tradition of strict legality running through the British system of government. Secondly, the rule of law embodies the principle of equality before the law: 'the universal subjection of all classes to one law administered by the ordinary Courts.' Disputes are to be adjudicated in accordance with a common set of rules, applied to ordinary subjects and Ministers of the Crown alike. The third sense of the rule of law is more elaborate. It embodies the conviction that the constitution itself comes from the ordinary law of the land. The 'law of the constitution', Dicey states, is 'not the source but the consequence of the rights of individuals'. Civil liberty is achieved not by the formal declaration of rights, but as a result of constant struggle and vigilance leading to outcomes recorded and protected in particular judicial decisions.

This safeguarding of liberty through the workings of the 'rule of law' contrasts sharply with the modern practice of formal

declarations of rights, in which rights to personal liberty derive—
are *deduced*—from the constitution. In the English case, however,
'constitutional principles' are *induced* from various court rulings
on personal rights. For Dicey, the English approach is clearly
preferable. Being the work of many 'whose labours gradually
framed the complicated set of laws and institutions which we call
the Constitution', it may form a less than tidy arrangement. The
Habeas Corpus Acts 'declare no principle and define no rights', but
they are 'for practical purposes worth a hundred constitutional
articles guaranteeing individual liberty'.

The reason is to be found in institutional arrangements. When the
source of personal liberty is located in written constitutions, those
rights can be suspended or repealed. But where the 'right to
individual freedom is part of the constitution because it is part of
the ordinary law of the land', Dicey contended that 'the right is
one which can hardly be destroyed without a thorough revolution
in the institutions and manners of the nation'. As the product of
long struggle that has become institutionalized in the practices of
governing, the English tradition of civil liberty is assumed to be
protected by strong shores. In Dicey's view, 'the securities for
personal freedom are in England as complete as the laws can
make them'.

Rule by law

The principle of the rule of law seems opposed to the fundamental
doctrine of parliamentary sovereignty. Since Parliament has
absolute authority in law-making, how can we know that
legislation inimical to liberty will not be passed? Dicey recognized
the problem but claimed that in two important ways parliamentary
sovereignty actually supports the rule of law. The first is that the
commands of Parliament must be approved by its constituent
parts, i.e. the Commons, the Lords, and the Royal Assent. This
process promotes deliberation and ensures that Parliament will
look 'with disfavour and jealousy on all exemptions of officials

from the ordinary liabilities of citizens or from the jurisdiction of the ordinary courts'. The second way is that legislation is strictly construed by judges, a tradition of legal formality that 'constantly hampers (and sometimes with great injury to the public) the action of the executive'. The courts 'will prevent, at any rate where personal liberty is concerned, the exercise by the government of any sort of discretionary power'. Parliament will confer broad powers only when absolutely necessary and a judiciary infused with the common law 'spirit of legality' will remain vigilant in interpreting restrictions on personal liberty.

In this tradition of constitutional thought, law is a species of command and since law imposes constraints, the less we have of it, the greater will be our freedom. This is the core of the British tradition of civil liberty: we appeal to our ancient liberties to protect us from the rigours of the law. The price of liberty is eternal vigilance: civil liberty is preserved in the British tradition by maintaining a vibrant political and parliamentary discourse. This is why freedom of the press is so highly prized. It is also why Parliament maintains extensive privileges with respect to freedom of speech, freedom from arrest, the ability to regulate its own proceedings, and the right to punish for breach of these privileges or for contempt of Parliament. And it helps us grasp the force of Montesquieu's claim that the 'state will perish when legislative power is more corrupt than executive power'.

Parliament's role is pivotal, but it must be assisted by a judiciary that applies the law strictly and in a way favourable to liberty. The judiciary's historic role is well illustrated by the landmark case of *Entick v Carrington* (1765), in which judges rejected the argument that a Minister's warrant was sufficient to authorize the search of premises and the seizure of papers alleged to contain evidence of seditious intent. Rebuffing the government's argument that this action was vital for reasons of state, the court claimed that 'the common law does not understand that kind of reasoning'. The judiciary explicitly rejected the claim that official status was sufficient of itself to confer lawful authority. 'If it is law', the judges declared, 'it will be found in our books. If it is not found there, it is not law.'

Crucial to Dicey's conception of the rule of law is the partnership between Parliament and judiciary. This partnership gives expression to a peculiarly British version of the separation of powers, a notion most clearly expressed in the words of Lord Diplock in *Duport Steels v Sirs* (1980): 'It cannot be too strongly emphasized that the British constitution, though largely unwritten, is firmly based on the separation of powers: Parliament makes the laws, the judiciary interprets them.'

Dicey illustrated this partnership by reference to the way the Habeas Corpus Act of 1679 put the common law writ on a statutory foundation. But this example also highlighted a potential weakness because, although the writ of habeas corpus—in denying the crown any inherent power of detention— had performed an important role in the 17th-century struggles, its continuing usefulness came to depend on parliamentary restraint. The difficulty has been that once parliamentary supremacy over the crown was confirmed by the 1688 Revolution and the Bill of Rights, Parliament became much more sanguine about conferring executive powers by statute. In one of its very first post-Revolution Acts (1 W&M c. 2), for example, the king was granted power to 'apprehend and detain such persons as He shall find just cause to suspect are conspiring against the Government'. In the following century, similar statutory powers drastically reduced the effectiveness of habeas corpus to protect even those who sought reform of the constitution rather than the revolutionary overthrow of the government.

This problem was experienced with dramatic effect in 19th-century Ireland, where a series of Acts granting wide powers of arrest and detention were passed. Burke had prophesied that authoritarian rule abroad might eventually corrupt liberal practices at home and this 19th-century Irish practice did indeed provide a model for the drafting of wartime emergency legislation during the 20th century. Legislation such as the Official Secrets Act 1911, the Defence of the Realm Acts 1914–15, and the Emergency Powers Act 1920 contained extensive powers of search, seizure, and detention alongside restrictions on freedom of speech, expression, and movement. The principle of the 'rule of law' extolled by Dicey had come to mean 'rule by such law as Parliament enacts'. And subsequent statutes, such as the Public Order Act 1936, the Criminal Justice and Public Order Act 1994, and successive Prevention of Terrorism Acts from 1974 have considerably undermined Dicey's confident assertion that Parliament will look 'with disfavour and jealousy on all exemptions of officials from the ordinary liabilities'.

But what of judicial protection? The record of the judiciary during much of the 20th century with respect to personal liberty has been mixed. The tone was set early on in cases such as *R. v Halliday, ex parte Zadig* [1917], where the judiciary departed from a strict construction to reject habeas corpus challenges to the legality of detaining persons of 'hostile origin or associations'. Likewise, the judicial record with respect to social and industrial conflicts and restrictions on radical political movements has been particularly supine. This is exemplified by the case of *Duncan v Jones* (1936), which upheld the power of the police to criminalize assemblies by breaking up meetings that might lead to a breach of the peace. By the 1980s, cases of miscarriage of justice such as the Birmingham 6, the Guildford 4, the Maguire 7, and the Bridgewater 4 had cast serious doubts on the impartiality of the judiciary. So when the judiciary sought to maintain a ban on the reporting of the memoirs of a former MI5 officer in the *Spycatcher* saga, their claim to be acting as guardians of a 'constitution of liberty' seemed scarcely credible (see Figure 4).

From a legal perspective, however, the case that best illustrates the limitations of the common law method of protecting liberty is that

BOOKS AND ARTS

My country, Wright or wrong

SPYCATCHER. By Peter Wright. *Viking. 392 pages. $19.95*

> The Economist has
> 1.5m readers in 170
> countries. In all but one
> country, our readers
> have on this page a
> review of "Spycatcher",
> a book by an ex-MI5
> man, Peter Wright. The
> exception is Britain,
> where the book, and
> comment on it, have
> been banned. For our
> 420,000 readers there,
> this page is blank—and
> the law is an ass.

4. *The Economist's* review of *Spycatcher*, 25 July 1987

of *Malone v Metropolitan Police Commissioner* (1979). In an action that paralleled *Entick's* case, Malone brought an action against the police for tapping his telephone, the authorization for which had been granted by the Home Secretary purely by administrative action, i.e. without explicit legal authority. But Malone's action failed on the ground that interception took place on telephone lines outside Malone's property. Since there had been no interference with his property or other rights, it was not deemed unlawful. In the words of the judge: 'England is not a country where everything is forbidden except what is expressly permitted: it is a country where everything is permitted except what is expressly forbidden.' Such a broad permission seems one that the police and security services are particularly well placed to exploit. Whatever else it stands for, *Malone* demonstrates that the tradition of protecting liberties by way of 'ordinary law' had distinct limitations.

Liberty and the growth of administrative government

The personal liberty that Blackstone and Dicey both held dear was that enshrined in classical liberalism. Sometimes called negative liberty it expresses a 'freedom from' control by another. It is also a type of liberty that in 18th- and 19th-century Britain was enjoyed only by a very limited class of persons: male property-holders who had already acquired the right not to be taxed or governed without their consent. From the late 19th century, classical liberalism was challenged by a more radical liberal philosophy that sought equal liberty for all.

This new liberalism contained two main elements. First it promoted universal political rights, that is, the right of every individual to play an equal role in sending representatives to Parliament. Classical liberals were not necessarily opposed to this aim, but they remained fearful of what they called 'the tyranny of the majority', tending to embrace only a democracy that could be reconciled with what Dicey called our 'inherited traditions of aristocratic government'. The second was the achievement of conditions conducive to equal liberty for all. This objective was more challenging: it required action by government to improve education, health, and social security, thereby providing a platform of basic social and economic entitlements that could help citizens realize their full potential. This objective could hardly be achieved without passing legislation conferring discretionary powers on government agencies, action that was vehemently opposed by classical liberals. The promotion of equality by governmental action, they argued, of necessity undermined liberty and the rule of law.

When 20th-century Liberal and Labour governments sought to promote these positive objectives by legislative means, many raised concerns on constitutional grounds. This was destined to become one of the major constitutional controversies of the first half of the 20th century. For many, the judiciary's vigilance in quashing the innovative and sometimes radical policies of Labour-controlled local authorities merely highlighted the common law's inability to adapt to the modern democratic world. When in 1929 Lord Hewart, the Lord Chief Justice and head of the common law courts, published a book complaining that the acquisition of discretionary powers by the executive was undermining the principles of the constitution, the controversy reached fever-pitch. Never let it be said, he declaimed, 'that liberty and justice, having been won, were suffered to be abstracted, or impaired in a fit of absence of mind'.

Hewart's claim that the growth of governmental powers posed the threat of a 'new despotism' to rival that of the Stuarts in the 17th century may have been constitutional but it was also intensely political. After all, when as Solicitor-General he represented the government in *Zadig's* case, he had not seemed unduly troubled by wartime incursions on 'personal liberty'. Similarly, his later ruling as Chief Justice in *Duncan v Jones* (1936) in favour of broader police powers to restrict freedom of expression exhibited little concern about the breadth of discretionary powers he was then recognizing. Such apparently selective intervention led Harold Laski to conclude that, in the guise of providing constitutional oversight, the judiciary had become 'the unconscious servant of a single class in the community'. The inter-war record left a specific constitutional legacy: that of profound distrust in the judiciary's ability to act as (self-appointed) guardians of the constitution.

After the Second World War, the judiciary managed to focus the constitutional issues entirely on the challenge posed by the growth of administrative power. 'Our procedure for securing our personal freedom is efficient', asserted Lord Denning in his influential lectures on *Freedom under Law* (1947), but 'our procedure for preventing the abuse of power is not'. The judiciary set themselves the task of developing new procedures and principles for supervising the exercise of public powers conferred by the legislative action of Parliament.

Judicial progress in modernizing these principles and procedures of judicial review was slow and faltering. Even the breakthrough cases of the 1960s—on issues like review for errors of law, procedural unfairness, and prerogative powers—were followed very hesitantly during the following decade. This was perhaps not surprising, because such changes directly cut across aspects of common law practice. It was not until the 1980s that Lord Diplock, after almost twenty years on the bench, felt able to state that he regarded the progress made towards creating a system of administrative law as 'the greatest achievement of the English courts in my judicial lifetime'.

What Diplock meant by the creation of a 'system' was that the courts had brought the administrative powers of government under the overarching supervision of the common law courts. In order to achieve this, the judiciary made two radical changes. First, they replaced the traditional heads of judicial review (natural justice, jurisdiction, *Wednesbury* unreasonableness) with markedly more rationalist tests (fairness, legality, irrationality). Secondly, the judiciary recognized that traditional adherence to the ordinary law had to be jettisoned in favour of a conceptual distinction between public law and private law.

Once these procedural and conceptual reforms had been introduced, the judges felt emboldened to involve themselves directly in constitutional modernization. They saw their essential task as that of bolstering the status of the rule of law within a modern constitutional framework. As traditionally formulated, the rule of law expressed a rule of political prudence which sheltered within the overarching framework of parliamentary sovereignty. The judicial challenge was to convert the rule of law from political aspiration into juridical principle. Having taken the first steps by reformulating the heads of judicial review, they later felt emboldened to assert that, rather than being a secondary feature of the constitution, the rule of law states its fundamental legal principle.

It is now recognized that an important step towards this claim was taken by Lord Bridge in *X. v Morgan-Grampian* (1991), a case involving a journalist's refusal to reveal who had supplied him with a confidential business plan (and therefore one not dealing centrally with relationships between government institutions). Holding that the maintenance of the rule of law is just as important to contemporary society as the democratic franchise, Bridge went on to assert that the rule of law 'rests upon twin foundations: the sovereignty of the Queen in Parliament in making the law and the sovereignty of the Queen's courts in interpreting and applying the law'. On one reading, this is no more than a reformulation of Diplock's classic account of separation of powers. But Bridge's use of the expression 'sovereignty' confounded settled understanding. In a conventional sense, his statement is nonsensical. Sovereignty is an absolute concept: to divide it is to destroy it. But this, it has since been assumed, was Bridge's objective: presenting traditional formulations in a completely different way makes innovative re-conceptualization possible. In relativizing the respective claims of Parliament and judiciary to make and interpret law, Bridge was pressing home the point that the overarching principle of the British constitution is not sovereignty but legality.

The judiciary has felt able to make this point explicitly only in the new millennium. In *R. v Home Secretary, ex parte Simms* [2000], for example, Lord Hoffmann noted that although the courts acknowledge the sovereignty of Parliament, they nonetheless 'apply principles of constitutionality little different from those which exist in countries where the power of the legislature is expressly limited by a constitutional document'. And in *Jackson v Attorney-General* [2005], Lord Hope confidently took the next step by making the stark claim that 'the rule of law enforced by the courts is the ultimate controlling factor on which our constitution is based'. He left amplification to Lord Steyn. 'The classic account given by Dicey of the doctrine of the supremacy of Parliament', Steyn asserted in *Jackson*, 'can now be seen to be out of place in the modern United Kingdom.' Parliamentary supremacy (the word he used in preference to sovereignty) may still be the general principle. But since it was created by the judges, he explained, 'it is not unthinkable that circumstances could arise where the courts may have to qualify a principle established on a different hypothesis of constitutionalism'.

The claim that the judges *created* the principle, a key tenet of what has become known as 'common law constitutionalism', is highly controversial. In modern times, judges have certainly come to *recognize* the doctrine of parliamentary sovereignty; since it is the consequence of 300 years of intense political struggle leading to basic shifts in the sources of governmental authority, they could hardly do otherwise. But Steyn's assertion that the doctrine was created by the judiciary is revolutionary. Steyn is claiming the authority of an autonomous concept of 'legal constitutionalism'. Contrary to the views of those such as Dicey and Jennings who acknowledged the distinction between constitution and law and therefore the conventional nature of the category 'constitutional law' (discussed above in Chapter 2), Steyn and his fellow legal rationalists promote law over practice, a normative version of constitutional ordering over institutional description, and 'legal constitutionalism' over the inherited practices of the 'political constitution'.

From civil liberties to human rights

The telephone-tapping case of *Malone* provides the pivot on which to assess the significance of these judicial developments in the protection of liberties. The case throws into relief the limitations of the common law approach to civil liberties, and in particular the consequences of a failure to draw a distinction between public law and private law. In the constitutional architecture of continental Europe, erected on the distinction between public law and private law, Ministers and their agents are not free to do whatever they want unless there are specific legal restraints. That principle may be correct as a matter of private law, in which ordinary persons can do anything the law does not prohibit. But in public law the true principle is that official persons can only act where the law permits. Private persons may be holders of rights, but official persons are impressed with duties.

This distinction acquires a special significance in Malone's case because, having failed in the English courts, Malone took his grievance to the European Court of Human Rights (ECtHR). In 1951 the UK had ratified the European Convention on Human Rights, an international treaty that established a charter of civil and political rights which contracting states have pledged to respect. The treaty provides for dispute resolution primarily through the ECtHR, and from 1966 the UK government had accepted the right of individuals to petition the Court. In Malone's case, the Court ruled that the government's action was in breach of its duty under Article 8 of the Convention to maintain respect for the individual's private life and correspondence. Being in breach of its international obligations, the government introduced legislation that established a procedure for authorizing telephone tapping. This was contained in the Interception of Communications Act 1985 (now in the Regulation of Investigatory Powers Act 2000).

Malone's case was hardly unique: since 1966 there have been over 60 judgments of the ECtHR finding breaches by the UK. Many have led to landmark changes in the law, ranging from the extension of prisoners' rights to the abolition of corporal punishment in schools. But because Britain maintains a distinction between domestic law and international law, the civil rights expressed in the Convention were initially not directly enforceable in British law. Individuals were therefore obliged to exhaust their domestic remedies before petitioning the ECtHR. Similarly, the rulings of the Court could not be directly enforced; they were dependent on governmental action to bring about a change in the law.

The growing influence of European human rights law should be read alongside the domestic movement to rationalize the principles of judicial review and to apply them more actively to the supervision of governmental action. The domestic movement has resulted in the judiciary taking a more rights-based approach. Rather than taking the traditional approach of focusing on the authority of the public body to act, the judiciary now ask whether and to what extent there has been an interference with an individual right. Such an approach puts the onus on the public body to justify its action. Nevertheless, within a constitutional frame that views the judiciary as the precision instruments of parliamentary intention, there are distinct boundary limits to the pursuit of activism. And it was for this reason that during the 1990s so many leading judges publicly advocated the necessity of making the European Convention on Human Rights directly enforceable in domestic courts.

That objective was realized after the 1997 election of a Labour government when, as part of its programme of 'constitutional modernization', it introduced the Human Rights Act 1998. This Act, which came into full effect in October 2000, made provision for the enforcement in domestic law of the rights guaranteed by the European Convention on Human Rights.

The 1998 Act makes it 'unlawful for a public authority to act in a way which is incompatible with a Convention right' (s. 6). Additionally, section 3 requires all legislation to be interpreted 'in a way which is compatible with the Convention rights'. This imposes a powerful interpretative obligation on the judiciary, one that runs contrary to the 'plain meaning' approach traditionally adopted by the courts. The Act nevertheless adheres to the formal principle of parliamentary sovereignty. Thus, if legislation cannot be interpreted in such a manner as to render it compatible with Convention rights, the courts are not empowered to strike it down. They can only issue a declaration of incompatibility under section 4, which has no direct legal effect: the legislative provision remains in force, although the Act does authorize the government to use a fast-track procedure for introducing legislation to achieve compatibility.

A high-profile illustration of the way this declaratory power operates is seen in *A. v Secretary of State for the Home Department* [2004]. The main issue in this case was whether the courts could review the government's decision to derogate from Art. 5 of the ECHR (the right to liberty) for the purpose of establishing, in Part IV of the Anti-Terrorism, Crime and Security Act 2001, a regime of indefinite detention of foreign nationals suspected of being international terrorists and who—for legal or practical reasons—could not be deported. Asserting jurisdiction, the House of Lords issued a declaration that this regime was incompatible with the Art. 5 right to liberty. Accepting this ruling, the government repealed the offending provisions of the 2001 Act and in 2005 introduced a new Prevention of Terrorism Act, containing a more graduated system of detention, called control orders.

The *A.* case also highlights a more general issue, that of the institutional tensions that the Human Rights Act exacerbates. Conferral on the executive of counter-terrorist powers after 11 September 2001 has given rise to a series of challenges under the Act which, rather than promoting a partnership between Parliament and judiciary, have led to the issue of security and liberty being reconfigured as one of institutional struggle. These are some of the most difficult issues to balance in rights-based regimes and, from the outset, they have proved challenging and highly controversial.

The Human Rights Act has established a new regime of civil rights protection. These rights range from the right to life, liberty, security, and fair trial to protections over freedom of thought, expression, and assembly. The Act signals a shift away from constitutional protection of civil liberty by way of parliamentary restraint and strict judicial construction towards a framework in which the judiciary perform a leading role as guardian of enumerated rights. It has not been uncontroversial, especially among those who, looking over the 20th-century record, feel— along with Lord Devlin—that once judges move beyond the narrow methods of interpretation and 'looked for the philosophy behind the Act' they invariably find 'a Victorian Bill of Rights, favouring (subject to the observance of accepted standards of morality) the liberty of the individual, the freedom of contract, and the sacredness of property, and which was highly suspicious of taxation'.

On the whole the new generation of judges has managed to avoid the political bear-traps these fresh responsibilities inevitably set up. One reason is down to their use of a more rationalist proportionality-based review test. Since the court is evidently a public authority for the purpose of the Act, judges are now obliged to develop the common law in conformity with those rights, and this marks another step along the road to rationalization. This probably presages further basic changes in constitutional ordering, for beyond the practical and political challenges of rights protection lie some fundamental conceptual ambiguities arising from the need to reconcile this newly enhanced principle of legality with the tradition of parliamentary sovereignty. But one thing seems certain: contrary to Dicey's contention, the law of the constitution is now the source rather than the consequence of our rights.

Chapter 6
Whither the constitution?

> ...hard it is for high and stately buildings long to stand except
> they be upholden and staid by most strong shores, and rest
> upon most sure foundations.
>
> Jean Bodin, 1576.

Constitutional development

All states are constructed from above, and the British case is no
exception. The story begins with the brute fact of a kingly power
imposing its rule over a people. But such a power can sustain itself
only with the acceptance of those subject to this rule. How does
the original usurpation become acceptable? How, in other words,
is the exercise of that power rendered legitimate? In his classic
treatment of this issue, Max Weber noted that there are three
main sources of legitimacy: *charismatic*, which involves devotion
to the exemplary, even sacred, character of a leader; *traditional*,
involving acceptance of the authority of immemorial custom; and
the *rational*, entailing belief in the rightful nature of a ruler's
authority to make law. In the history of governmental forms, these
sources of legitimization follow a sequential arrangement, from
ancient to modern. They also suggest an ascending order of clarity,
from opaque to transparent.

In the story of British government, we have seen how monarchical power came to be accepted through four critical stages of development. The first stage was reached by distinguishing between the private and public aspects of kingship, between feudal overlordship and official rulership. In the second stage, the representative nature of the office of the king was recognized: this is an office held in trust for the public good. The third stage acknowledged its composite character incorporating the roles of law-making, law-enforcing, and law-interpreting and in so doing the necessity for the institutional differentiation of governmental functions between king's council, king's court, and king-in-Parliament was accepted.

Through such a process was the constitution created. The constitution is the arrangement through which both rulers and subjects express their beliefs about the authority of government. The British constitution has evolved from ancient to modern, from rudimentary to complex. It has also evolved from the charismatic, through the traditional, to the rational, though, as Bagehot's account illustrated, during the modern period it has blended these three elements in unusual ways.

But there is a further stage in this narrative of constitutional development. This is the recognition that, rather than being conceded from above, governmental authority is actually conferred from below, when it is accepted that authority derives not from the sacred character of the office, or from an acceptance of custom, but directly from the people. And herein lies the peculiarity of British constitutional development: this last stage of modernization has not been effected through juristic reconstruction, but through political accommodation.

As a result, the law of the constitution has retained its ancient form, under which the highest authority in the land is the Crown-in-Parliament. It is only through political practice that the legal powers of the crown have been stripped from the monarch and made accountable to the people. The powers of the crown are now exercised by Ministers who command the confidence of Parliament. The contest between political parties provides the means through which the queen's government is rendered accountable to Parliament. This party contest also becomes the vehicle for adapting governmental arrangements to the principle of democratic accountability. The British constitution provides for representative and responsible government. In the popular imagination, the highest authority in the land does not rest in the abstract concept of the Crown-in-Parliament: it is located in a Victorian Gothic palace on the banks of the Thames at Westminster.

The arrangement has worked well enough, especially in enabling the British to make the transition to democracy without violent rupture. The problem has been that during the 20th century its limitations were exposed and faith in these arrangements has been suffering a progressive decline. Unsure of our customs, we have been obliged to write down more and more of these practices in rules and regulations (Ch. 2). Confounded about its role with the emergence of big government, Parliament has become primarily a testing ground of ministerial competence and it would appear to retain its pivotal status only because the British lack the political imagination to conceive of alternative ways of constituting governmental authority (Ch. 3). Experiencing the growth of identity politics, the British no longer express confidence in themselves as a nation that forms a state (Ch. 4). Seeing a collapse of the tradition of protecting civil liberties through strict legality, we try to bolster liberty by adopting an off-the-peg set of civil rights (Ch. 5). Does a coherent set of rules, principles, and practices of governing any longer exist?

Constitutional interpretation

The authority of a constitution rests ultimately on the power of imagination, on the expression of a 'collective dream' about who we are as a nation and how we envision the nature of our governing arrangements. We regularly update these arrangements by statutory reform and other formal means. But to maintain its vibrancy, constitutional practice also needs the power of innovative re-interpretation. We have seen many illustrations of this process at work in this narrative history of the British constitution: British government has been able to modernize its arrangements while continuing to pay tribute to its ancient inheritance primarily through a practice of innovative re-interpretation. But have we reached a point where governmental developments now impose unbearable strains on any narrative coherence, when the discordant strands can no longer be drawn into a coherent story? Are we now at the stage at which customary practices are unable any longer to determine present behaviour or guide future conduct? Must the authority of experience now yield to the force of expectation?

The great constitutional scholars all derived their confidence from belonging to the Victorian era. Since then, we have never produced a narrator to match the imaginative authority of the Whig historians or of Bagehot and Dicey. And during the last quarter of the 20th century the dominant mood changed: the exercise of imaginative re-interpretation was abandoned in the face of what was seen as a pressing need for fundamental reconstruction. The politics of repair extolled by a line of commentators from Burke and Oakeshott was replaced by that of destruction and creation. As we are propelled into the 21st century, the constant refrain became that of 'constitutional modernization'.

Constitutional modernization

The topic of constitutional modernization is perplexing. Many believe that something as malleable as British governing arrangements scarcely deserves the epithet 'constitution'. Insofar as the term was used in 20th-century studies it was simply assumed that the constitution changed as the arrangements of government changed. But the mood of general dissatisfaction is now causing some to reflect on the overall architecture of British government, which has developed rather in the manner of an old building that has been constantly adapted, repaired, and renovated at different times and in different styles. Specifying an overall design for the arrangement is now almost impossible. But renovating to make it fit for contemporary use requires architects possessed with real vision. This is a challenging enough task for a single building; for an entire system of government, the chances of success do not seem high.

Consider, for example, the institution of Parliament. It is evident in the light of its history (Ch. 3) that it does not simply have a legislative role in some modern tripartite division of powers. Conceived as such its deficiencies soon reveal themselves. The first-past-the-post electoral system leads to an obvious skewing of its representational function. The adversarial mode in which its business is conducted ensures government dominance of the legislative timetable. The intense pressure on its timetable together with peculiarities of its meeting times severely limit opportunities for deliberative scrutiny, and its cramped working conditions impede informed discussion. But whenever we turn to the issue of reform, it is invariably the legislative model that looms into view. So after a Commons Modernization Committee was established in 1997, various reforms were instituted: streamlined procedures, more family-friendly sitting hours, and improved timetabling which meant that uncompleted Bills could be carried over from one session to the next. Such reforms have made MPs better equipped to carry out some of their tasks. But they have done so at the cost of blunting certain instruments, such as the threat to continue debate late into the night or to filibuster a Bill, that have often been most effective in forcing governments to pay attention to their concerns.

British constitutional practice works by holding governmental institutions and practices in a relationship of mutual tension. If the tension is relaxed, vital constitutional dimensions of the practice might be lost. This, for example, has been the story of central–local government relations since 1980, when central pressures in pursuit of efficiency began to destroy the sense of autonomy that provides the justification for local government (in contrast to local administration). We have experienced it also at the centre of government in the divide between a permanent, impartial civil service and transient, partisan ministers. Two agencies with different motivations, answerable to different constituencies and operating on different timescales, have to try and ensure that government decisions are clearly formulated and effectively implemented. A programme of modernization— opening up civil service recruitment, appointing special advisers, pursuing policy-making outside formal Whitehall processes, artificially dividing between policy and operations, hiving off tasks to private or arm's-length bodies—might make sense and deliver a government's agenda more speedily. But if the tension in relations between politicians and administrators is destroyed the costs can be substantial, not least those incurred by the loss of trust in government when things go wrong.

One of the difficulties in modernizing is that the logic of British constitutional practice is no longer widely understood, with the result that the law of unintended consequences often takes effect. Bringing in ministerial special advisers with the status of civil servants has blurred the distinction between official and politician and confused lines of accountability. Giving civil servants formal responsibility for decisions within the sphere of their operations has eroded the ability of Parliament to test ministerial performance. Making policy in bilateral ministerial meetings rather than in Cabinet might be speedier but it is less robust and diminishes the collective responsibility of government. Driven by the desire to improve governmental effectiveness, so-called modernization often results in fragmentation and confusion.

Even when the modernization programme is focused on removing more obvious anachronisms, there is still an evident unwillingness to address fundamentals. By all means modernize the monarchy by removing the rule of male-priority primogeniture, but removing religious discrimination in the law of succession? Perhaps that's a step too far. The monarchy bolsters government with the strength of religion, noted Bagehot, and 'when a monarch can bless it is best that she be not touched'. Mess with the protocols and the magic is lost. Subjecting the monarchy to a modern calculus of economy, efficiency, effectiveness, and equity is the surest way to its destruction.

It is not just the fate of one family that is at stake. In the slipstream of the royal train are any number of titles, privileges, and honours with political as well as social significance. Here the entity of most obvious constitutional relevance is the House of Lords. How can a self-styled modern democratic legislature, it was often asked, persist with a second chamber dominated by hereditary peers? When the Parliament Act 1911 limited the powers of the Lords, its preamble stated the future intention to 'substitute for the House of Lords as it at present exists a Second Chamber constituted on a popular instead of hereditary basis'. No action to make good on that pledge ever materialized and during the 20th century it seemed that the Lords, poorly attended and sitting only a couple of days a week, would slowly die through debility. That belief was confounded in 1958 by the enactment of the Life Peerages Act. This reform enabled the leaders of the main parties to stuff the House with patronage appointments, since when more than 1,000 life peers have been appointed. The reform had its progressive dimension: for the first time, women could participate in the House in significant numbers. But its main impact has been to rejuvenate the trade in political honours, to strengthen the power of party leaders, and to increase the power of an entirely unelected chamber.

Reforms were enacted in the House of Lords Act 1999, which removed the right of hereditary peers to sit but then authorized them to elect ninety-two of their number to represent their interests in the House. This was supposed to be the first step towards more comprehensive reform but subsequent proposals reached stalemate over questions of composition and mode of membership. This remained the case until the Coalition Agreement of 2010, which included a provision for establishing a wholly or mainly elected second chamber. A Reform Bill designed to remove hereditary peers, though not bishops of the Church of England, and to establish a majority of elected members, was introduced in June 2012. However, because of a failure to elicit the required support, especially among Conservative backbenchers, in August the Bill was withdrawn. Among the current uncertainty, we can be assured of one thing: modernizing reforms are unlikely to take effect any time soon.

More than a century after an expressed intention to introduce a popularly elected second chamber, the House of Lords remains, consisting of the 92 hereditary peers (now the only elected element!), 26 archbishops and bishops of the Church of England (all male), and over 500 appointed life peers. This saga highlights the problem of leaving constitutional reform to government, since governments have no incentive to enhance the legitimacy of an institution that could restrain its power.

While the agenda of constitutional modernization remains in the hands of the government, any implementation will be subject to the exigencies of the government of the day. There is no obvious solution. The language of constitutional reform will always just be, in Ferdinand Mount's fine phrase, 'the poetry of the politically impotent', while responsibility for implementation of reform rests with those who acquire no benefit.

The common law constitution

There is one institution of government well placed to take advantage of the prevailing mood of modernization in order to enhance its status and prestige: the judiciary. The declining authority of conventional practices during the last half of the

20th century means that the lack of formal institutional safeguards has been acutely felt. An increasing unease about the workings of traditional constitutional arrangements is one of the factors behind the growth of judicial review. The declining efficacy of parliamentary remedies has been perceived by the judiciary as falling well short of what was needed 'to bring the performance of the executive into line with the law' and to meet 'the minimum standards of fairness implicit in every Parliamentary delegation of a decision-making function'. In order to avoid an accountability gap, Lord Mustill explained in 1995, 'the courts have had no option but to occupy the dead ground in a manner, and in areas of public life, which could not have been foreseen 30 years ago'.

We saw in the last chapter how the courts have moved beyond the phase of activism in judicial review of governmental action to a more explicit attempt to re-order constitutional fundamentals. Their objective has been to rid themselves of the legacy of a Victorian mentality that maintained that judges sit merely 'as servants of the Queen and the legislature' (Willes J, 1871) and to resurrect a juristic account of the British constitution founded on 'common law constitutionalism'. Invoking the spirit of the ancient constitution, this movement requires significant innovative re-interpretation of 'the law of the constitution'. The constitution, it is suggested, is not some ineffable entity to be glimpsed fleetingly through various laws and practices. It is nothing other than a body of 'fundamental law' that exists to ensure that government operates in a manner that preserves liberty. It is, they are suggesting, 'in its essentials the creation of the common law' and it now falls to the judiciary to unpack the constitution as an ordered system of principles.

This is a bold undertaking involving a theoretical shift of revolutionary proportions. The common law is no longer to be seen as moving from precedent to precedent, nor is it intrinsically subservient to statute. The notion of the common law is to be thoroughly rationalized. The inevitable consequence is that the concept of law that shapes judicial practice is transformed. The concrete becomes abstract, precedent turns into principle, the protection of liberties is converted into the promotion of liberty, and jurisdictional control is replaced by legality as the fundamental legal principle of the constitution. The old 'constitution of liberty' becomes a new 'constitution of legality'.

The 'common law constitution' thesis has been presented most explicitly by Sir John Laws, a leading Court of Appeal judge, who claims that sovereignty does not lie with 'those who wield governmental power' but rests 'in the conditions under which they are permitted to do so'. It is 'the constitution, not the Parliament' that is sovereign. Laws follows through the logic of this claim by arguing that these conditions must now be made explicit as 'a framework of fundamental principles'. This is a task for the judiciary, whose constitutional role must be to act as 'the guarantee that this framework will be vindicated'.

This the courts are now doing. They assert that there are such things as 'fundamental constitutional rights' which the judiciary must be vigilant to protect. These include rights of participation in the democratic process, equality of treatment, freedom of expression, the right to a fair trial, and the right of unimpeded access to the court. Judges contend that they will vigilantly protect these rights, which cannot be overridden by Act of Parliament unless that intention is expressed in the clearest of terms. The courts have also begun to differentiate between statutes, creating a new category of so-called constitutional statutes. Constitutional statutes are those that either regulate the relationship between citizen and state or enlarge or diminish the scope of fundamental constitutional rights. In this category fall Magna Carta, the Bill of Rights 1689, the Treaty of Union 1707, the Representation of the People Acts, the European Communities Act 1972, the Human Rights Act 1998, and the Scotland and Wales legislation of 1998. With respect to these constitutional statutes, the judiciary is saying that amendment or repeal must be effected by Parliament in explicit terms; such changes are not to be imputed or presumed.

The enterprise of establishing a 'constitution of legality' is a work-in-progress and its full implications are yet to be revealed. But it has already acquired some support from parliamentary sources. The term 'constitutional law' is not recognized as a technical category. Consequently, although Parliament has commonly passed constitutional legislation for dependent jurisdictions—the Commonwealth of Australia Constitution Act 1900, the Bermuda Constitution Act 1967, and even the Northern Ireland Constitution Act 1973 offer illustrations—it has shied away from arrogating to itself the authority of declaring the meaning of the British constitution. So whenever it has sought to change constitutional arrangements Parliament has done so indirectly and in purely technical language, such as in the Representation of the People Acts or the Parliament Acts.

Only in the aftermath of the constitutional modernization programme do we encounter legislation that explicitly states its intention to 'reform the constitution'. The first such is the Constitutional Reform Act 2005, which sought to institutionalize a new understanding of the separation of powers. Since judges had become routinely involved in the review of governmental action, it seemed anachronistic to some that the highest court, the Appellate Committee of the House of Lords, remained part of the legislature and its judges, the Law Lords, could debate legislation that might subsequently become the subject of litigation. Although the judiciary had, by convention, maintained its distance from the executive and the legislature, the government concluded this was no longer sufficient. It proposed the establishment of a new Supreme Court for the UK as a formal expression of the principle of separation. This was enacted in Part III of the 2005 Act, and in Part II the opportunity was also taken to specify certain of the conventions on judicial independence in statutory form.

In certain respects, the establishment of the Supreme Court was a typically British reform: the existing Law Lords simply upped sticks and, at great expense, moved out of the Palace of Westminster and into newly refurbished accommodation across Parliament Square. But great efforts have been made to heighten the symbolic significance of the move: the Justices took the initiative in modernizing the working arrangements of the court, especially with respect to layout, costume, and accessibility. In place of the Baconian image of judges as lions under the throne, 'circumspect that they do not check or oppose any points of sovereignty', we are offered a new court emblem: a wreath of entwined vegetation symbolizing the four nations of the UK with not a crown in sight.

By such means do modest reforms assume a greater significance. The formation of the Supreme Court on the principle of separation supports the judiciary's venture of articulating their newly discovered fundamental principles of the constitution. And the 2005 Act provides an additional gloss. In a remarkable innovation, section 1—apparently included as a result of judicial lobbying— states that the Act 'does not adversely affect...the existing constitutional principle of the rule of law'. The rule of law is formally recognized by Act of Parliament as a 'constitutional principle'. It is evidently the sort of principle whose meaning only the judiciary is equipped to determine. We are perhaps only a short step away from the American aphorism that 'we are under a Constitution, but the Constitution is what the judges say it is'.

Prospects

We can finally offer an answer to the question: does Britain possess a constitution? The answer is that the traditional idea of a constitution which the British have long celebrated has become so corroded that it no longer provides a coherent account of the nature of British government. The programme of constitutional modernization implemented since 1997 has done little to improve this situation. In formalizing and rationalizing elements of governmental practice, it has resulted in the further erosion of conventional understandings, raising as many questions as it manages to answer. But politics abhors a vacuum. Steadily moving in to fill this void has been the judiciary, with its unique, incrementally staged modern version of a constitution expressed as a framework of fundamental law.

This is a narrative in the early stages of telling. As Laws L J put it in 2002: 'In its present state of evolution, the British system may be said to stand at an intermediate stage between parliamentary supremacy and constitutional supremacy.' While the judiciary's goal evidently is that of establishing 'constitutional supremacy', what that constitution will look like remains unclear. What is clear is that, rather late in the day, the British are attempting to establish a constitutional framework in accordance with a modern template. Whatever its precise content, this will be a constitution that lawyers have made. And in this respect it will accord with the standard trajectory of constitutional development.

When traditional sources of legitimacy dissipate, when deference to 'natural' aristocracies or to customary ways of doing things ceases, new ways of justifying government have to be found. Modern government is of necessity the preserve of elites, in that it falls to a relatively small group, the political class, to carry on the activity of governing. But once natural aristocracies lose their power, who is able to perform that role? The answer, first offered by Tocqueville, is that this task can be assumed only by lawyers. Belonging 'to the people by birth and interest, and to the aristocracy by habit and taste', lawyers are uniquely able to straddle the two groups. Presenting themselves as advocates for the people, they share in common with aristocracies 'the same instinctive love of order and formalities, and they entertain the same repugnance to the actions of the multitude'. Lawyers are particularly well placed to reconcile competing demands of order and freedom, Tocqueville explained, since although they value freedom they 'are attached to public order beyond every other consideration'. It is to lawyers that we must turn when we champion principles of liberty and equality while accepting the necessity of hierarchy. Lawyers are the conduits of modern constitutional democracy.

One of the distinctive features of the traditional British constitution has been the manner in which lawyers have been confined to the performance of certain vital but limited tasks. This is destined to change. Even in the mid-19th century Tocqueville noted that in the American system there was hardly a political question that was not transformed into a judicial question. This has been the general experience of modern constitutional democracies, in which the language of law comes to colonize the discourse of politics. Whether or not the ideal of the 'rule of law' is ever realized, we surely end up with the rule of lawyers.

For the British, it would appear that a new chapter in constitutional history is being opened. In one sense, this exercise is being undertaken in a thoroughly British manner: rather than starting afresh, we are creating a modern-style constitution in an incremental and pragmatic fashion. This new style of constitution is certainly intended, just as Lord Hailsham advocated in the 1970s, to be written and protected by law. This prompts a number of questions about the politics of lawyers and judges. Will this development lead to a restoration of the 'constitution of liberty' in the classical liberal sense or can we formulate new conceptions of liberty for the contemporary age? Once the language of law colonizes the field of constitutional politics, how can we address concerns raised by writers such as Marquand and Hutton about the need to rejuvenate a public realm to protect social democratic values of solidarity and common citizenship? Should we really be entrusting such constitutional questions to a judiciary stocked with lawyers who, far from having engaged with the challenges of contemporary government, will have spent their professional lives mainly in lucrative practice at the commercial bar? And so we end just as we began, not with answers but with a new set of questions. As one chapter of constitutional development draws to a close, we look forward with a mixture of anxiety and anticipation to the prospect of reading the new.

Further reading

Introduction

Lord Hailsham, *The Dilemma of Democracy: Diagnosis and Prescription* (Glasgow: Collins, 1978).

David Marquand, *The Unprincipled Society: New Demands and Old Politics* (London: Fontana, 1988).

Will Hutton, *The State We're In* (London: Cape, 1995).

Chapter 1: What constitution?

The traditional idea of the constitution

G. W. F. Hegel, *The Philosophy of Mind* [1830], trans. W. Wallace (Oxford: Clarendon Press, 1971), § 540.

Edmund Burke, *Reflections on the Revolution in France* [1790], ed. C. C. O'Brien (London: Penguin, 1986). An edition is available at: <http://www.constitution.org/eb/rev_fran.htm>.

Nevil Johnson, *In Search of the Constitution: Reflections of State and Society in Britain* (Oxford: Pergamon Press, 1977).

The modern idea of the constitution

James Madison, Alexander Hamilton, and John Jay, *The Federalist Papers* 1787, ed. I. Kramnick (London: Penguin, 1987). An edition is available at: <http://avalon.law.yale.edu/subject_menus/fed.asp>.

Thomas Paine, *Rights of Man, Common Sense and Other Political Writings*, ed. M. Philp (Oxford: Oxford University Press, 1995).

An edition is available at: <http://www.constitution.org/tp/rightsman1.htm>.

Traditional v. modern

US Constitution 1787, available at: <http://avalon.law.yale.edu/18th_century/usconst.asp>.

C. H. McIlwain, *Constitutionalism: Ancient and Modern* (Ithaca, NY: Cornell University Press, rev. edn. 1947), available at: <http://www.constitution.org/cmt/mcilw/mcilw.htm>.

Francis D. Wormuth, *The Origins of Modern Constitutionalism* (New York: Harpers, 1949), available at: <http://www.constitution.org/cmt/wormuth/wormuth.htm>.

M. J. C. Vile, *Constitutionalism and the Separation of Powers* (Oxford: Clarendon Press, 1967), available at: <http://oll.libertyfund.org/?option=com_staticxt&staticfile=show.php%3Ftitle=677>.

Zachary Elkins, Tom Ginsburg, and James Melton, *The Endurance of National Constitutions* (Cambridge: Cambridge University Press, 2009).

Why does Britain not possess a modern constitution?

Alexis de Tocqueville, *Democracy in America* [1835], trans. H. Reeve, introd. D. J. Boorstin (New York: Vintage Books, 1990), 2 vols. An edition is available at: <http://oll.libertyfund.org/index.php?option=com_staticxt&staticfile=show.php%3Ftitle=2284&Itemid=28>.

Steve Pincus, *1688: The First Modern Revolution* (New Haven: Yale University Press, 2009).

E. S. Morgan, *Inventing the People: The Rise of Popular Sovereignty in England and America* (New York: Norton, 1989).

T. B. Smith, 'The Union of 1707 as Fundamental Law' (1957) *Public Law* 99–121.

Neil MacCormick, 'Does the United Kingdom Have a Constitution?' (1978) 29 *Northern Ireland Legal Quarterly* 1–20.

The spirit of the British constitution

Edmund Burke, 'On the Present Discontents' (1770), available at: <http://www.econlib.org/library/LFBooks/Burke/brkSWv1c1.html>.

Michael Oakeshott, *Rationalism in Politics and Other Essays* (London: Methuen, 1962).

Chief Justice Coke, *Twelfth Reports, Prohibitions del Roy* (1607) 12 *Co. Rep.* 63.

Sir Alfred Denning, 'The Spirit of the British Constitution' (1951) 29 *Canadian Bar Review* 1180–95.

Philip Allott, 'The Theory of the British Constitution', in Hyman Gross and Ross Harrison (eds.), *Jurisprudence: Cambridge Essays* (Oxford: Clarendon Press, 1992), 173–205.

Chapter 2: Writing the constitution

Authority and liberty

Montesquieu, *The Spirit of the Laws*, trans. and ed. A. Cohler, B. Miller, and H. Stone (Cambridge: Cambridge University Press, 1989). Bk. 11, ch. 6. An edition is available at: <http://www.constitution.org/cm/sol.htm>.

J. L. De Lolme, *The Constitution of England, or, An Account of the English Government* (Indianapolis: Liberty Fund, 2008), available at: <http://oll.libertyfund.org/index.php?option=com_staticxt&staticfile=show.php%3Ftitle=2089>.

Rudolf von Gneist, *History of the English Constitution* (London: Clowes, 1886).

Josef Redlich, *The Procedure of the House of Commons* (London: Constable & Co., 1908).

The Norman Yoke and the Gothic Bequest

Edward Coke, *The Selected Writings and Speeches of Sir Edward Coke*, ed. Steve Sheppard (Indianapolis: Liberty Fund, 2003), vol. 2.

James I, 'Speech to Star Chamber of 20 June 1616', in his *Political Writings*, ed. J. P. Somerville (Cambridge: Cambridge University Press, 1994), 204–28.

E. A. Freeman, *The Growth of the English Constitution* (London: Macmillan, 1876), quoted at p. 57.

J. G. A. Pocock, *The Ancient Constitution and the Feudal Law: A Study of English Historical Thought in the Seventeenth Century* (Cambridge: Cambridge University Press, rev. edn. 1987).

Christopher Hill, 'The Norman Yoke', in his *Puritanism and Revolution* (London: Secker & Warburg, 1958), 50–122.

Herbert Butterfield, *The Whig Interpretation of History* (London: Bell, 1931).

J. W. Burrow, *A Liberal Descent: Victorian Historians and the English Past* (Cambridge: Cambridge University Press, 1981).

Blackstone's *Commentaries*

William Blackstone, *Commentaries on the Laws of England* (Oxford: Clarendon Press, 1776), vol. 1, available at: <http://avalon.law.yale.edu/subject_menus/blackstone.asp>.

John W. Cairns, 'Blackstone, an English Institutionalist: Legal Literature and the Rise of the Nation State' (1984) 4 *Oxford J. of Legal Studies* 318–60.

J. C. D. Clark, *The Language of Liberty 1660–1832* (Cambridge: Cambridge University Press, 1994), esp. ch. 1.

Dicey on the *Law of the Constitution*

A. V. Dicey, *Introduction to the Study of the Law of the Constitution* (London: Macmillan, 8th edn., 1915), available at: <http://oll.libertyfund.org/index.php?option=com_staticxt&staticfile=show.php%3Ftitle=1714&Itemid=27>.

Bagehot on *The English Constitution*

Walter Bagehot, *The English Constitution* (Oxford: Oxford University Press, 2001). An edition is available at: <http://www.gutenberg.org/ebooks/4351>.

S. Collini, D. Winch, and J. W. Burrow, *That Noble Science of Politics: A Study in Nineteenth-Century Intellectual History* (Cambridge: Cambridge University Press, 1983), ch. 5.

Twentieth-century constitutional writing

F. W. Maitland, *The Constitutional History of England* (Cambridge: Cambridge University Press, 1908), 526–7 (constitutional law not a technical term).

W. I. Jennings, *The Law and the Constitution* (London: University of London Press, 1933).

W. I. Jennings, *Cabinet Government* (Cambridge: Cambridge University Press, 1936), quoted at p. xii.

W. I. Jennings, *Parliament* (Cambridge: Cambridge University Press, 1939).

W. I. Jennings, *Local Government in the Modern Constitution* (London: University of London Press, 1933).

John P. Mackintosh, *The British Cabinet* (London: Stevens, 1962), quoted at p. 524.

J. A. G. Griffith, Editorial, 1963 *Public Law* 401.

Ferdinand Mount, *The British Constitution Now* (London: Heinemann, 1992), ch. 2 'The Three Simplifiers' [Bagehot, Dicey, and Jennings].

Nevil Johnson, *In Search of the Constitution* (1977), ch. 3 'The Waning of Constitutional Understanding', quoted at p. 33.

Nevil Johnson, *Reshaping the British Constitution: Essays in Political Interpretation* (Basingstoke: Palgrave Macmillan, 2004).

Codifying conventions

Vernon Bogdanor, *The New British Constitution* (Oxford: Hart, 2009).

Ministerial code: <http://www.cabinetoffice.gov.uk/sites/default/files/resources/ministerial-code-may-2010.pdf>.

Civil Service Management Code: <http://resources.civilservice.gov.uk/wp-content/uploads/2011/09/CSMC-June-2011.doc>.

Committee on Standards in Public Life: <http://www.public-standards.gov.uk/>.

Independent Parliamentary Standards Authority: <http://parliamentarystandards.org.uk/Pages/default.aspx>.

Cabinet Manual: <http://www.cabinetoffice.gov.uk/sites/default/files/resources/cabinet-manual.pdf>.

Peter Hennessy, *The Hidden Wiring: Unearthing the British Constitution* (London: Gollancz, 1995).

Anthony King, *The British Constitution* (Oxford: Oxford University Press, 2007).

Institute of Public Policy Research, *A Written Constitution for the United Kingdom* (London: Mansell, 1993).

Richard Gordon, *Repairing British Politics: A Blueprint for Constitutional Change* (Oxford: Hart, 2010).

Vernon Bogdanor, *The Coalition and the Constitution* (Oxford: Hart, 2011).

Chapter 3: Parliamentary government

Origins of Parliament

John Le Patourel, *The Norman Empire* (Oxford: Clarendon Press, 1976).

J. C. Holt, *Magna Carta* (Cambridge: Cambridge University Press, 2nd edn., 1992).

A. F. Pollard, *The Evolution of Parliament* (London: Longmans, 1920).

Parliament and the formation of the state

G. R. Elton, *The Tudor Revolution in Government* (Cambridge: Cambridge University Press, 1953).

Christopher Hill, *The Century of Revolution, 1603–1714* (London: Routledge, 2nd edn., 2001).

Charles I, 'XIX Propositions made to both Houses of Parliament to the King's Most Excellent Majesty: With His Majesty's Answer', in J. L. Malcolm (ed.), *The Struggle for Sovereignty: Seventeenth Century English Political Tracts* (Indianapolis: Liberty Fund, 1999), vol. 1, 145–78.

The modern constitutional settlement

E. S. Morgan, *Inventing the People: The Rise of Popular Sovereignty in England and America* (New York: Norton, 1989).

John Brewer, *The Sinews of Power: War, Money and the English State, 1688–1783* (New York: Knopf, 1989).

Steve Pincus, *1688: The First Modern Revolution* (New Haven: Yale University Press, 2009).

Democratization

Edmund Burke, 'Thoughts on the Present Discontents' (1770), available at: <http://www.gutenberg.org/files/2173/2173-h/2173-h.htm>.

Edmund Burke, 'Speech to the Electors of Bristol' (1774), available at: <http://www.gutenberg.org/files/15198/15198-h/15198-h.htm#ELECTORS_OF_BRISTOL>.

G. W. F. Hegel, 'The English Reform Bill', in his *Political Writings*, trans. T. M. Knox (Oxford: Clarendon Press, 1964), 295–330.

Iain McLean, *What's Wrong with the British Constitution?* (Oxford: Oxford University Press, 2010), ch. 4.

Dicey, *Law of the Constitution*, Introduction to 8th edn., quoted at pp. xciii–xciv.

Modern parliamentary practice

Bagehot, *The English Constitution*, ch. 5.

Robert Blackburn and Andrew Kennon, *Griffith and Ryle on Parliament: Functions, Practice and Procedures* (London: Sweet & Maxwell, 2nd edn., 2003), statistics on legislation at p. 400.

Geoffrey Marshall, *Constitutional Conventions: The Rules and Forms of Political Accountability* (Oxford: Clarendon Press, 1984).

R. H. S. Crossman, 'Introduction' to Bagehot, *The English Constitution* (Glasgow: Collins, 1963).

Peter Hennessy, *Cabinet* (Oxford: Blackwell, 1986).

Tony Wright, 'What are MPs for?' (2010) 81 *Political Quarterly* 298–308.

Report of the Inquiry into the Circumstances Surrounding the Death of Dr David Kelly CMG, Session 2003–4, HC 247 (Hutton Report): <http://www.the-hutton-inquiry.org.uk/content/report/>.

Review of Intelligence on Weapons of Mass Destruction, HC Session 2003–4, HC 898 (Butler Report): <http://www.archive2.official-documents.co.uk/document/deps/hc/hc898/898.pdf>.

The Iraq Inquiry (Chilcot Report): <http://www.iraqinquiry.org.uk/>.

Chapter 4: The expansion and contraction of the English state

England, Britain, United Kingdom

R. R. Davies, *The First English Empire: Power and Identities in the British Isles, 1093–1343* (Oxford: Oxford University Press, 2000).

Colin Kidd, *Union and Unionisms: Political Thought in Scotland, 1500–2000* (Cambridge: Cambridge University Press, 2008).

Colin Kidd, 'The Matter of Britain and the Contours of British Political Thought', in David Armitage (ed.), *British Political Thought in History, Literature and Theory, 1500–1800* (Cambridge: Cambridge University Press, 2006).

Linda Colley, *Britons: Forging the Nation, 1707–1837* (New Haven: Yale University Press, 2005).

Neil MacCormick, *Questioning Sovereignty* (Oxford: Oxford University Press, 1999), ch. 4.

McLean, *What's Wrong with the British Constitution?* Pt. II, Bonar Law quoted at p. 114 and Dicey at p. 132.

Dicey, *Law of the Constitution*, quoted at p. 445.

Gerald Aylmer, 'The Peculiarities of the English State' (1990) 3 *Journal of Historical Sociology* 91–108.

Empire

Sir John R. Seeley, *The Expansion of England* (London: Macmillan, 1925), quoted at pp. 51, 10.

Uday Singh Mehta, *Liberalism and Empire: A Study in Nineteenth-Century British Liberal Thought* (Chicago: University of Chicago Press, 1999).

Philip J. Stern, *The Company State: Corporate Sovereignty and the Early Modern Foundations of the British Empire in India* (Oxford: Oxford University Press, 2011).

Sir Frederick J. D. Lugard, *The Dual Mandate in British Tropical Africa* (Edinburgh: Blackwood, 1922).

Eric Stokes, *The English Utilitarians and India* (Oxford: Oxford University Press, 1989).

European Union

H. Gaitskell, Speech as Leader of the Labour Party to the Labour Party Conference, 1962, available at: <http://www.cvce.eu/obj/speech_hugh_gaitskell_october_1962-en-05f2996b-000b-4576-8b42-8069033a16f9>.

Costa v ENEL, Case 6/64 [1964] ECR 585.

Van Gend en Loos v Nederlandse Administratie der Belastingen Case 26/62 [1963] ECR 1.

R. v Secretary of State for Transport, ex parte Factortame (No. 2) [1991] 1 AC 603.

Sir William Wade, 'Sovereignty: Revolution or Evolution?' (1996) 112 *Law Quarterly Review* 568–75.

T. R. S. Allan, 'Parliamentary Sovereignty: Law, Politics, and Revolution' (1997) 113 *Law Quarterly Review* 443–52.

R. Daniel Kelemen, *Eurolegalism: The Transformation of Law and Regulation in the European Union* (Cambridge, Mass.: Harvard University Press, 2011).

Devolution

Owen Dudley Edwards (ed.), *A Claim of Right for Scotland* (Edinburgh: Polygon, 1989).

Vernon Bogdanor, *Devolution in the United Kingdom* (Oxford: Oxford University Press, 2001).

Richard W. Rawlings, *Delineating Wales: Constitutional, Legal and Administrative Aspects of National Devolution* (Cardiff: University of Wales Press, 2003).

Brigid Hadfield, 'Devolution: A National Conversation?', in Jeffrey Jowell and Dawn Oliver (eds.), *The Changing Constitution* (Oxford: Oxford University Press, 7th edn., 2011), ch. 8.

The Belfast Agreement 1998, Cm. 3883.

State, nation, and citizen

Martin Loughlin, 'The State, the Crown and the Law', in Maurice Sunkin and Sebastian Payne (eds.), *The Nature of the Crown: A Legal and Political Analysis* (Oxford: Oxford University Press, 1999), ch. 3.

Calvin's Case (1608) 7 Co. Rep. 1.

Ann Dummett and Andrew Nicol, *Subjects, Citizens, Aliens and Others: Nationality and Immigration Law* (London: Weidenfeld & Nicolson, 1990).

Chapter 5: Civil liberty

The constitution of liberty

Blackstone, *Commentaries*, Bk. I, ch. 1.

Montesquieu, *Spirit of the Laws*, Bk. 11, ch. 5.

Dicey, *Law of the Constitution*, chs. 4 and 8.

Rule by law

David Clark and Gerard McCoy, *The Most Fundamental Legal Right: Habeas Corpus in the Commonwealth* (Oxford: Clarendon Press, 2000), esp. ch. 2.

Entick v Carrington (1765) 19 St. Tr. 1030.

Duport Steels v Sirs [1980] 1 All ER 529, at 541 per Lord Diplock.

R. v Halliday, ex p. Zadig [1917] AC 260.

Duncan v Jones [1936] 1 KB 218.

Malone v Metropolitan Police Commissioner [1979] Ch 344.

Conor Gearty, *Civil Liberties* (Oxford: Oxford University Press, 2007).

Keith Ewing and Conor Gearty, *The Struggle for Civil Liberties: Political Freedom and the Rule of Law in Britain, 1914–1945* (Oxford: Oxford University Press, 2000).

Liberty and the growth of administrative government

A. V. Dicey, *Lectures on the Relation between Law and Public Opinion in England during the Nineteenth Century* (London: Macmillan, 1905), quoted at p. 58.

Lord Hewart, *The New Despotism* (London: Benn, 1929).

H. J. Laski, 'Judicial Review of Social Policy in England' (1926) 39 *Harvard Law Review* 832–48, quoted at p. 848.

Alfred Denning, *Freedom under the Law* (London: Stevens, 1949), quoted at p. 126.

R. v I.R.C., ex parte National Federation of Self Employed [1982] AC 617, at 641 per Lord Diplock.

X. v Morgan-Grampian [1991] 1 AC 1.

R. v Home Secretary, ex parte Simms [2000] 2 AC 115, at 131 per Lord Hoffmann.

Jackson v AG [2005] UKHL 56.

From civil liberties to human rights

Malone v UK (1984) 7 EHHR 14.

A. v Secretary of State for the Home Department [2004] UKHL 56.

Lord Devlin, 'The Judge as Lawmaker' (1976) 39 *Modern Law Review* 1–19.

Sir Stephen Sedley, 'The Sound of Silence: Constitutional Law without a Constitution' (1994) 110 *Law Quarterly Review* 270–91.

Tom Bingham, *The Rule of Law* (London: Penguin, 2011).

J. A. G. Griffith, *The Politics of the Judiciary* (London: Fontana, 5th edn., 1997).

Chapter 6: Whither the constitution?

Constitutional development

Max Weber, *Economy and Society*, ed. G. Roth and C. Wittich (Berkeley and Los Angeles: University of California Press, 1978), 26–56, 212–26.

Max Weber, 'The Profession and Vocation of Politics', in his *Political Writings*, ed. Peter Lassman and Ronald Spiers (Cambridge: Cambridge University Press, 1994), 309–69.

Constitutional modernization

House of Commons Modernization Committee, *Modernisation of the House of Commons: A Reform Programme*, HC 1168, Session 2001–2.

Martin Loughlin, 'The Demise of Local Government', in Vernon Bogdanor (ed.), *The British Constitution in the Twentieth Century* (Oxford: Oxford University Press, 2003), 521–56.

Public Administration Select Committee, *Taming the Prerogative: Strengthening Ministerial Accountability to Parliament*, HC 422, 4th Report, Session 2003–4.

C. D. Foster, *British Government in Crisis* (Oxford: Hart, 2005).

House of Lords reform: House of Lords Reform Bill, HC Bill 52, Session 2012–13: <http://services.parliament.uk/bills/2012-13/houseoflordsreform/documents.html>.

Mount, *The British Constitution Now*, quoted at p. 2.

The common law constitution

R. v Secretary of State for the Home Department, ex parte Fire Brigades Union case [1995] 2 AC 513, per Lord Mustill.

Lee v Bude & Torrington Junction Railway (1871) LR 6 CP 576, per Willes J.

Sir John Laws, 'Law and Democracy' 1995 *Public Law* 72–93, quoted at p. 92.

Charles Evan Hughes, 'Speech before Elmira Chamber of Commerce, 3 May 1907', in his *Addresses, 1906–1916* (New York: Putnams, rev. edn., 1916), 179–93, quoted at p. 185.

T.R.S, Allan, *Law, Liberty and Justice: The Legal Foundations of British Constitutionalism* (Oxford: Oxford University Press, 1994).

Thomas Poole, 'Back to the Future? Unearthing the Theory of Common Law Constitutionalism' (2003) 23 *Oxford J. of Legal Studies* 435–54.

Prospects

Secretary of State for the Home Department v Roth [2002] 1 CMLR 52, para. 71 Laws LJ.

Tocqueville, *Democracy in America*, vol. 1, ch. 16.

Index

SOCIAL MEDIA
Very Short Introduction

Join our community
www.oup.com/vsi

- Join us online at the official Very Short Introductions **Facebook** page.
- Access the thoughts and musings of our authors with our online **blog**.
- Sign up for our monthly **e-newsletter** to receive information on all new titles publishing that month.
- Browse the full range of Very Short Introductions online.
- Read **extracts** from the Introductions for free.
- Visit our library of **Reading Guides**. These guides, written by our expert authors will help you to question again, why you think what you think.
- If you are a teacher or lecturer you can order inspection copies quickly and simply via our website.

Visit the Very Short Introductions website to access all this and more for free.
www.oup.com/vsi